Academic Mini-Lectures

A Text for Listening and Note-Taking Practice

Connie Roguski
University of Kansas,
Applied English Center

Edith Palmberg
Olathe District Schools, Number 233,
Olathe, Kansas

Maxwell Macmillan
International Publishing Group

TO ALL STUDENTS WHO HAVE EXPRESSED
A DESIRE TO BE BETTER NOTETAKERS.

Library of Congress Cataloging-in-Publication Data

Roguski, Connie.
    Academic mini-lectures : a text for listening and note-taking
practice / Connie Roguski, Edith Palmberg.
        p.   cm.
    ISBN 0-02-403130-5
    1. College readers.   2. English language—Textbooks for
foreign speakers.   3. Listening.   4. Note-taking.   5. Study,
Method of.
I. Palmberg, Edith.   II. Title.
PE1122.R55   1990
438.3′4—dc20   89-34904
                                                        CIP

Collier Macmillan Canada, Inc.

Editor(s): Maggie Barbieri
Production Supervisor: Anne Reifsnyder
Production Manager: Sandra Moore
Text Designer: N. S. G. Design
Cover Designer: Jane Edelstein
Cover photograph: The Stock Market
Illustrations: G & H Soho, Ltd.

Photo Credits
Page 2: Courtesy of International Business Machines Corpora-
tion.   **Page 12:** Courtesy of the University of Kansas Office of
University Relations. Photographer: Steve Dick.   **Page 20:** Eric
Liebowitz.   **Page 36:** Pascal James Imperato.   **Page 46:** Cour-
tesy of the University of Kansas Office of University Relations.
Photographer: Steve Dick.   **Page 52:** Courtesy of the University
of Kansas Office of University Relations.   **Page 58:** Courtesy of
the University of Kansas Office of University Relations. Photog-
rapher: Diane Dultmeier.   **Page 66:** Gamma-Liaison/Smith,
Grafton.   **Page 74:** Cornell Capa/Magnum.   **Page 84:** Sona
Doran.   **Page 94:** Gamma-Liaison/Jordan, Peter.
Page 104: Sona Doran.   **Page 114:** Sona Doran.
Page 122: Connie Roguski.

This book was set in Times Roman by V&M Graphics, Inc.,
printed and bound by Viking Press Inc.
The cover was printed by Phoenix Color Corp.

Printing: 1 2 3 4 5 6 7   Year: 0 1 2 3 4 5 6

Maxwell Macmillan International Publishing Group
ESL/EFL Department
866 Third Avenue
New York, NY 10022

Printed in the U.S.A.

ISBN   0-02-403130-5

Acknowledgments

Many people deserve thanks for their contributions to this book.

For inspiration on the work itself, thanks to Danny Horowitz for his work on identifying academic needs of international students, and to Jack Richards for his article on listening comprehension, which reminds us of the numerous micro-skills needed to follow lectures.

We thank the fourteen speakers who gave very generously of their time despite demanding schedules. They recorded and sometimes rerecorded the mini-lectures, discussed their own lecturing styles, and told us about the needs of students in their classes.

For excellent seminars on study skills, thanks to the staff of the Student Assistance Center at the University of Kansas for helping undergraduates succeed.

At the Applied English Center at the University of Kansas, classroom instructors and students shared their honest reactions to the materials at different stages of readiness. For his insights and help with the writing of the math lesson, we heartily thank Michael Bowen. Sarah Sistrunk, Loretta Flanagan, and Julie Bruch ruthlessly checked and double-checked the scripts and vocabulary. We also thank our colleagues whose encouragement and support kept us motivated during the long process, especially Elizabeth F. Soppelsa, O. Dean Gregory, Margaret P. Coffey, and Chuck Seibel.

At Harvard University in the Summer ESL Program, we thank Anne Dow and William Biddle for their encouragement, and the instructors and students for their enthusiasm for materials that came from real lecturers.

In the production of the audiotapes, many professionals played a part. We thank the Ermal Garinger Academic Resource Center at the University of Kansas for its support of this project. In particular, in the early editing of the tapes, James A. Hogg showed great patience and professionalism. Carl Hoffman, formerly of Ramona Studios, Lawrence, Kansas, provided technical expertise and early editing of the audiotapes. Mark Marek, City Spark Studios, Kansas City, Missouri, provided expert supervision of the final editing of the audiotapes.

In the production of the text and teacher's materials, we had the help of two tireless workers. Thanks to Anneliese Simmons for her hours of typing and lively suggestions about the note-taking exercises. We also thank David Byrd for his practice note-taking and work on the vocabulary for the instructor's manual. At Macmillan, we would like to thank Kathy Niemczyk for her guidance with the editing and production, and Mary Jane Peluso and Maggie Barbieri for their editorial help.

Thanks to Connie's family and friends: her mother, Katherine, for her contagious love of reading and learning; her late father, Emil, for his hard work and creative spirit; her sister, Pat, for her constant encouragement; and her brother, Rick, for many friendly discussions on this and other projects. And thanks to her friends, Ron Tippie, who helped keep the task in perspective, and Alice Lachman, who offered cheer in the home stretch.

Thanks to Edith's family and friends: her husband, Thane, and sons, Britton and Wade, for their support and understanding of her preoccupation during the development and completion of the project; her father, Edgar Soule, for his intellectual curiosity and cheerful nature; and late mother, Ruth Soule, for her love and support, as well as her physical and mental toughness. And thanks to her friend and colleague, Nancy Marie Wood, for her support during the good and bad times.

C.R.
E.P.

Contents

Contents

Introduction

Academic Mini-Lectures: A Text for Listening and Note-Taking Practice is a university-level text primarily for students of English as a second or foreign language. The text is designed as a bridge between the simplified listening material sometimes used in beginning and intermediate courses and the more complex, generally much longer, lecture samples used in advanced textbooks. This text will also be useful for any native speakers who need to develop the skills necessary to take notes from lectures, speeches, or other types of presentations delivered at normal speed.

Speakers

The text consists of fifteen mini-lectures. Each one is given by an expert in a different academic field. Most of the speakers are university professors. There are eleven lessons done by male speakers and four by females. Although most of the speakers are from the University of Kansas, they represent diverse backgrounds and accents, thus giving students a sampling of what they may hear in university classes. The fields represented range from music therapy, art history, and math to electrical engineering, physics, and botany. This variety will offer students and teachers the opportunity to listen to and discuss information from many fields.

Sequence of the Lessons

Each speaker chose to explain a topic or concept often covered in introductory-level courses. The mini-lectures were audiotaped in the professors' offices and transcribed later. The lectures appear in the text in an order that reflects their complexity and length. Lessons 1–4 are lectures of less than three minutes. The focus of these early lectures is more limited than that of the later ones. Lessons 5–10 give the students practice with longer material that is still limited in scope. Lessons 11–15 are more challenging because they are four to five minutes in length and include several rhetorical patterns that students must be able to distinguish to take notes.

Skills Practiced

Richards (1983) has suggested a range of micro-skills students need for successful academic listening. This text will address many of these skills, including identifying the scope and development of a lecture; recognizing key vocabulary related to the topic; recognizing cohesion devices; and listening for voice cues such as stress, pauses, rising intonation, and speed.

Exercise Format

The three main areas of practice in this text are (1) listening for the organization of ideas and key information in the lectures and recording this in note form; (2) developing strategies for reviewing these notes; and (3) using the scripts to look at features of the lectures in greater detail to become aware of the devices used by professors as they explain concepts.

Introduction

The exercises for each lesson were selected to prepare the beginning notetaker to function more successfully in an academic setting. There are prelistening and postlistening activities that allow students to place the lecture content into the framework of their own knowledge. Most of the following exercises will be included in every lesson. A few will be omitted when not appropriate for the content of the lecture.

1. *Speaker*   This section establishes the speaker's expertise. Students will read information about the speaker's academic degrees and areas of specialization.

2. *Background*   The students must be cognitively prepared for each lecture. For students whose knowledge of the content area is limited, the background section gives a short overview of the topic. Pictures, charts, and diagrams offer more contextual support.

3. *Prelistening Discussion*   The questions in this section encourage the exchange of knowledge that is so often possible with people of varied experience. The questions or statements provided here will broaden the cognitive framework of the students before they hear the specific information in the lectures.

4. *Prelistening Vocabulary*   This section appears in every lesson and is crucial to the success of the note-taking. Students are asked to give synonyms or other forms of the word so that they have the chance to review and use vocabulary they may have seen or heard in another context without resorting to a bilingual dictionary for each item. For each new word, the syllable with primary stress is indicated with capital letters to help students recognize this word when they hear it.

General — This section includes words that could be used in any discipline as well as in everyday conversation. These words should be the ones that students try to include in their active vocabulary.

Field-specific — Terms in this section are primarily used in a specific field. Recognition of these terms is necessary for the lectures, but students need not remember all these technical terms.

Defined by the lecturer — In a few lessons, there are vocabulary items that professors define in the lectures. An additional context is given for students to guess at the meaning.

Idioms — In several lessons, the professors use idioms that would be difficult for students to understand without some preparation. Students are given short contexts to read, and teachers elicit the meaning of the idioms from the students.

5. *Main Idea/Organization Check*   Before listening to the lecture, the student is asked to preview some questions. As they listen to the lecture for the first time, the students answer multiple-choice questions that guide them through the organization of the lecture. This helps them anticipate what will come next and focus in on transitions used by the lecturer. In some lessons, students will prepare their own preview questions.

6. *Note-Taking Techniques*   The goal of this text is to provide beginning notetakers with a variety of approaches to the task of writing notes while listening to a lecture. In each lesson, one to three techniques will be introduced. Students first practice them in short contexts given by the teacher. With the actual mini-lecture, students have a partially filled-in note-taking guide page to complete. This page resembles a notebook page with adequate blank space for notes during both the listening activity and the discussion. Later, students are encouraged to listen to the lecture again and take their own notes on another piece of paper. We hope that after using this text students will be able to choose the techniques that best match their learning styles and fields of study.

7. *Review Strategies*   This section provides students with opportunities and techniques to reorganize and review their notes in preparation for quizzes and tests.

8. *Features of the Lecture*   A speaker's voice, personality, and topic together create a certain lecturing style. Some features of each speaker's presentation will be pointed out. These include intonation, speed, pauses, focus cues, rephrasings, fillers, extended examples, and use of passive or conditionals to make a point. The students' task is to follow along with the lecture by reading the transcript and actively making note of the features being studied. This analysis will interest students with varying levels of aural comprehension.

9. *Comprehension Exercise:* True/False   The questions in this section deal with specific details of the lectures. They give an indication of the students' knowledge of the topic at a certain point in time. The questions could be done earlier in the lesson without the benefit of notes. The students could also use their notes to answer the questions and then reevaluate their notes to see what else they might need to include and where it should be written.

10. *Comprehension Exercise:* Short essay   These questions can be used for review, group or pair discussion, or in-class written quizzes. Horowitz (1986) has suggested incorporating more academic tasks into the work that students do as they are studying English. If students keep their notes, review them for several weeks, and then prepare for a quiz on the material, they will understand more easily the need to take complete notes. These short essay questions also give students the chance to practice their writing skills by synthesizing information they have learned from these lectures. According to Peterson (1986), this task is one of the most difficult for both native and non-native speakers of English.

11. *Discussion or Written Assignments*   The assignments in this final section of each lesson allow the students and teachers many opportunities to explore the general content of the lectures. These assignments include in-class speeches, group discussions, role plays, individual projects, library assignments, field trips, and personal essays.

We hope that students who are beginning to take notes on academic lectures will feel a sense of accomplishment while they work through the variety of material in this text of mini-lectures given by real professors. We also expect that this practice will enable international students to approach longer lectures more confidently.

References

Horowitz, D. 1986. What professors actually require: Academic tasks for the ESL classroom. *TESOL Quarterly* 20:445–462.

Peterson, P. W. 1986. Strategies in listening and notetaking: Four perspectives. Paper presented at symposium, Listening Colloquium. TESOL Conference, Anaheim, California.

Richards, J. C. 1983. Listening comprehension: Approach, design, and procedure. *TESOL Quarterly* 17:219–240.

To the Student

What Are Mini-Lectures?

In this text you will hear speakers from several different fields giving very short lectures. These mini-lectures are similar to the explanations a professor might give when a student asks a question in class or during office hours. These mini-lectures might also be introductions to new topics. Each one is only about three to five minutes long.

When students take their first academic course at English-speaking universities, they often have trouble understanding the lectures. This may happen because the professors speak quickly and use some unfamiliar words and expressions. Sometimes it takes a while to adjust to the professor's lecturing style.

Where Did the Lectures Take Place?

We recorded the lectures in the speakers' offices. If you hear some background noise on the tapes, it is not a mechanical problem. We intended to leave the noise (i.e., bus, telephone, air-conditioning) so that you will have a realistic challenge. In some lecture auditoriums and classrooms, there may also be some distracting noise that makes it hard for you to hear the professor. These speakers did not write out their lectures. They were speaking only from notes as they might do when they teach their classes. Some students have never heard this kind of unsimplified English before. You will not be able to catch every word or phrase in the lectures. Don't worry.

Why Do Students Need to Learn to Take Good Notes?

One important skill that university students need is the ability to take organized, accurate notes in classes. It is also important to develop a system for reviewing and expanding your class notes. This helps you when you are preparing for classes and studying for quizzes and exams.

Will I Need to Write Many Notes?

Native speakers don't listen for every word during a lecture. Instead, they focus on key words that are stressed or repeated. They also listen for paraphrasing, saying the same idea with different words. They listen for examples. This is the information that they put in their notes.

What Kind of Paper Will I Need?

In most chapters of this text, you will have an incomplete note-taking guide page in the text, and you can use a blank page of your own for a second practice. Most note-taking guide pages in the text are divided into two parts. The two-thirds of the page on the right side is for your class notes. Many students use paper that is divided this way. It is called "law ruled," and you can buy tablet or spiral-bound notebooks with this type of paper or you can draw lines to divide blank paper. The margin on the left one-third of the page gives you a place where you can write practice test questions. These notes can remind you to ask the instructor a question in class or can help you review for a quiz.

What Will I Learn?

After you have completed this book, you will know many new ways to take notes and to organize material. While you are improving in these areas, you will also develop many of the listening skills that are necessary for successful note-taking in academic classes: catching the main idea, following the development of a lecture, understanding the examples given, recognizing a restatement of an idea, and noticing changes in the lecturer's voice to show emphasis.

Other Resources with Suggestions on Note-Taking

Dubin, Fraida. *How to Succeed in Your College Courses: A Guide for the ESL Student.* New York: Association of American Publishers, Inc., 1983.

Heiman, Marcia and Joshua Slomianko. *Predicting Exam Questions.* Cambridge, Mass.: Learning Skills Consultants, 1979.

Kesselman-Turkel, Judi and Franklynn Peterson. *Test-taking Strategies.* Chicago: Contemporary Books, Inc., 1981.

Yorkey, Richard. *Study Skills for Students of English.* New York: McGraw-Hill, 1982.

LESSON

1 / Spreadsheets

A. Speaker

Herb Harris is the Assistant Director for User Service for the Academic Computing Services Center at the University of Kansas. He has a bachelor's degree in philosophy from Yale University and a master's degree and doctorate in linguistics from the University of Kansas.

B. Background

Throughout the world, computers are becoming a part of our lives. This speaker talks about how the microcomputer is making our lives easier. He tells what a spreadsheet is and how we use it to make our personal and business lives less complicated.

C. Prelistening Discussion

1. Have you ever used a computer? Where?
2. Can you think of some uses for a microcomputer in our daily lives?
3. Has the microcomputer changed your life? How?

D. Prelistening Vocabulary

When you listen to a lecture, even if it is very short, you may hear many words that are new to you. Before you listen to each lecture in this text, you will have some practice with the key vocabulary words that you will need to recognize in order to understand the lecturer's ideas. Primary stress is in capital letters.

The vocabulary work is divided into several sections. In each lesson, you will find a general vocabulary section, which includes very common words that may be used in many different fields of study and in everyday conversation. You should study these basic words carefully. You may already know another form of the word. For example, if the general word is *unemployment*, you may already know the word *employer*. You can use your knowledge of these other forms to help you guess the meaning of the new word from the context that the lecturer uses.

The second section of the vocabulary work is field-specific because you will find words or phrases that are more often used in a specific field such as architecture, music, electrical engineering, or economics. You will need to understand these terms for the lecture, but it is not necessary to spend much time studying these words unless the lecture is in your own field of study.

In some lessons, there will be a third section for vocabulary that is defined in the lecture or for idioms used by the speaker. It is important to learn how to listen for these definitions and explanations that you will hear.

General   *Read the sentence for each word. For* **synonyms**, *think of another word or other words that could replace the italicized word. For* **other forms**, *write in nouns, adjectives, or any other word forms of the italicized word.*

1. label   The *label* on the cereal box lists the ingredients.
   (LAbel)

   SYNONYMS: *tag, slip*

   Other forms: *labeler*

3

2. expenditures
   (exPENditures)

The great *expenditures* of money caused many problems for the business.

SYNONYMS: _____

Other forms: _____

3. automatically
   (autoMATically)

He *automatically* looks for his mail when he gets home.

SYNONYMS: _____

Other forms: _____

4. variable
   (VARiable)

A *variable* number will change from formula to formula.

SYNONYMS: _____

Other forms: _____

Field-specific   *For each of the following words, read the sentence and use the context to guess the definition. Write the meaning in your own words if possible.*

5. microcomputer
   (microcomPUTer)

The *microcomputer* is a small computer that is helpful to businesses.

MEANING: _____

6. spreadsheet
   (SPREADsheet)

A *spreadsheet* is one way a microcomputer can show figures.

MEANING: _____

7. matrix
   (MAtrix)

A *matrix* contains rows and columns.

MEANING: _____

8. dynamism
   (DYnamism)

The computer program showed *dynamism*; when I changed one amount, the total was different.

MEANING: _____

E. Note-Taking Techniques: 1. Listing Main Points
2. Understanding a Table

1. Listing Main Points

When you are in lecture classes, you will want to write the main ideas down quickly. Later you may want to look over your notes carefully and reorganize them by main points and details. This is *one* way of taking notes, and it is not necessarily the best way for you. You do need to be able to take notes in different ways, depending on the subject and the way the speaker presents the material.

Try to write down the main points of a short paragraph that your teacher will read to you. Then go over the main points with your classmates.

_____

_____

_____

_____

_____

_____

_____

2. Understanding a Table

Look at the spreadsheet in Table 1–1. Answer and then discuss the following questions about the spreadsheet.

1. How many rows and how many columns are there?
2. What was the ending balance for June?
3. Whose family budget does this spreadsheet describe?
4. How much money did the Romanos plan to put in their savings account in February?
5. How could this spreadsheet help a family with their budget planning?

Table 1–1. Spreadsheet

JOHN & SUSAN ROMANO
FAMILY BUDGET
JANUARY–JUNE 1991

	JAN	FEB	MAR	APR	MAY	JUNE
Balance FWD	$1,562.75	$1,198.96	$590.17	$506.38	$557.59	$544.80
John's Income	1,200.00	1,200.00	1,200.00	1,200.00	1,200.00	1,200.00
Susan's Income	1,350.00	1,350.00	1,350.00	1,350.00	1,350.00	1,350.00
Rent	(500.00)	(500.00)	(500.00)	(500.00)	(500.00)	(500.00)
Gas	(70.00)	(65.00)	(40.00)	(35.00)	(30.00)	(30.00)
Water	(22.00)	(22.00)	(22.00)	(22.00)	(22.00)	(22.00)
Lights	(35.00)	(35.00)	(35.00)	(30.00)	(25.00)	(25.00)
Telephone	(50.00)	(50.00)	(50.00)	(50.00)	(50.00)	(50.00)
Cable TV	(22.74)	(22.74)	(22.74)	(22.74)	(22.74)	(22.74)
Groceries	(300.00)	(300.00)	(300.00)	(300.00)	(300.00)	(300.00)
Auto Expenses	(150.00)	(150.00)	(150.00)	(150.00)	(150.00)	(150.00)
Life Insurance	(50.39)	(50.39)	(50.39)	(50.39)	(50.39)	(50.39)
Auto Insurance		(100.00)				
Health Insurance	(33.66)	(33.66)	(33.66)	(33.66)	(33.66)	(33.66)
Home Insurance					(124.00)	
Clothing	(100.00)	(100.00)	(100.00)	(100.00)	(100.00)	(100.00)
Entertainment	(75.00)	(75.00)	(75.00)	(75.00)	(75.00)	(75.00)
Gifts	(50.00)	(50.00)	(50.00)	(50.00)	(50.00)	(75.00)
Miscellaneous	(200.00)	(200.00)	(200.00)	(200.00)	(200.00)	(200.00)
Student Loan	(55.00)	(55.00)	(55.00)	(55.00)	(55.00)	(55.00)
Mastercard	(200.00)	(150.00)	(100.00)	(75.00)	(75.00)	(75.00)
Money Market	(900.00)	(900.00)	(850.00)	(750.00)	(700.00)	(800.00)
Savings Acct	(100.00)	(300.00)	0.00	0.00	0.00	0.00
Ending Balance	$1,198.96	$590.17	$506.38	$557.59	$544.80	$531.01

◎◎ F. Main Idea/Organization Check

Read through these questions or statements before you listen to the tape. As you listen to the lecture for the first time, listen for the main ideas. Circle the letter of the best answer.

This is not a note-taking exercise. You will have a chance to take notes on the material later.

1. According to the lecture, the microcomputer revolution developed partly because of the _____.
   a. spreadsheet
   b. computer chip
   c. technological advances

2. The elementary form of a spreadsheet is _____, which makes it very useful for business and personal use.
   a. a list of five columns
   b. a matrix of rows and columns
   c. a set of five rows and columns

3. Harris describes _____ kinds of information that we can find in a cell of a spreadsheet.
   a. 3
   b. 4
   c. 2

4. The _____ of a spreadsheet is one thing that caused the business community to use it.
   a. instability
   b. dynamism
   c. variability

◎◎ G. Note-Taking Guide Page

Listing Main Points

As you listen to the tape again, try to fill in the main points and other information of the lecture on page 7. If you do not get all the information this time, listen to the tape again.

G. Note-Taking Guide Page

Main Topic: _Spreadsheets_

1. Spreadsheets — business wanted microcomputers

2. Elementary form _____

3. Each cell _____ types information

4. _____ info _____

5. Number — monetary amt., date, _____

6. Formula — makes it _____

Formal Outline

I. Spreadsheets

   A. Business community impact

      1. Microcomputer revolution

II. Organization of spreadsheet

   A. Elem. form

      1. _____

   B. Three types of inform. in each cell

      1. _____

         a. Label of rows and columns

         b. Example — budgets

      2. _____

         a. Monetary, date, _____

      3. Formula

         a. Makes _____

         b. This sold to business community

H. Review Strategy: Reorganizing Notes into a Formal Outline

A formal outline has this general form.

I. Main Topic

  A. Subtopic

    1. Main point (information)

      a. Detail

      b. Detail

    2. Main point (information)

      a. _____

      b. _____

  B. Subtopic

    1. _____

      a. _____

      b. _____

    2. _____

      a. _____

      b. _____

II. Main Topic

  A. _____

    1. _____

      a. _____

      b. _____

    2. _____

      a. _____

      b. _____

  B. _____

    1. _____

a. _____

b. _____

2. _____

  a. _____

  b. _____

The number of main topics, subtopics, main points, and details will vary from lecture to lecture, but this is the general form that a formal outline will take.

Look over your notes on page 7. Reorganize the main points and other information into a formal outline.

I. Features of the Lecture: 1. Repetition
                                                  2. Linking Expressions

1. Repetition

An important feature of the Harris lecture is the use of repetition and linking expressions. For example, he says ". . . the business community *found a use* for microcomputers and since they *found a use* . . ." He repeats key information in another way so that the listener will be sure to hear it.

2. Linking Expressions

He also uses such words as *so* and *for example* to connect his ideas.
Turn to the script for Harris on page 133 and follow the directions given.

J. Comprehension Exercise: True/False

Use your notes to decide whether each of the following statements is *true* or *false*. If the statement is *false*, underline the information that is incorrect. Change this information so that the statement will be true, according to the lecture. Circle *T* for true and *F* for false.

1.   *T*   *F*   The spreadsheet was very useful to the business community, especially for budgets.

2.   *T*   *F*   The spreadsheet concept comes from Michigan University.

3.   *T*   *F*   Three types of information are in the spreadsheet.

4.   *T*   *F*   The spreadsheet is sometimes dynamic.

5.   *T*   *F*   If you change one number, you must calculate the change in every part of the spreadsheet.

K. Comprehension Exercise: Short Essay

Choose one of the following topics. Write a paragraph using information from your notes.

1. Summarize the information from your formal outline in a paragraph or two.
2. Describe the three types of information on a spreadsheet and give examples for each.

L. Discussion or Written Assignments

1. What are the effects of microcomputers in your daily life? In groups, develop a list of situations where computers are used in everyday life. Try to list as many different uses as possible.

2. How have microcomputers changed your nation? the world?

3. Are there other uses for the microcomputer that could help your nation and the world?

4. What kind of problems do we have now as a result of microcomputer technology?

5. Find an article in a newspaper or weekly magazine about computers, and write a short report for the teacher or make an oral report to the class.

Discussion Notes

_____

_____

_____

_____

_____

_____

_____

_____

_____

_____

_____

_____

_____

_____

_____

GIFT OF
THE CLASS OF

2/ Demographics of International Students in the United States

A. Speaker

Clark Coan is Associate Dean of Student Life and Director of the Office of Foreign Student Services at the University of Kansas, a post he has held since 1957. He holds a doctorate from Kansas in social science education and has served on many national commissions, task forces, and in various associations concerned with international intercultural exchange. He is a past president of the National Association for Foreign Student Affairs.

B. Background

In different areas of the United States, there are English as a Second Language programs for international students. These programs are usually located on campuses of universities or colleges. On most campuses there is an office with staff who help international students with various problems regarding admission, housing, and academic work.

C. Prelistening Discussion

1. What are the students like who study English in the United States? Are they undergraduate or graduate students? What are their majors?
2. In Intensive English programs in the United States, where do you think most students are from?
3. What do you think most students in these programs have as their major?

D. Prelistening Vocabulary

Before you listen to the lecture, practice the pronunciation of the following key words with your teacher. Notice the syllable in each word with the most important stress.

General   *Read the sentence for each word. For **synonyms**, think of another word or other words that could replace the italicized word. For **other forms**, write in nouns, adjectives, or any other word forms of the italicized word.*

1. statistics
   (staTIStics)

   People read *statistics* to understand the relationship between two or more things. This knowledge helps us predict future situations.

   SYNONYMS: *numbers, figures*

   Other forms: *statistical, statistically*

2. funding
   (FUNDing)

   The money to finance any major project is called *funding*.

   SYNONYMS: _____

   Other forms: _____

3. significant
   (sigNIFicant)

   He made *significant* progress during the semester; his grade went from a 70-percent to a 90-percent average.

   SYNONYMS: _____

   Other forms: _____

4. impact   Computers have made a tremendous *impact* on education in
   (IMpact)   recent years.

   SYNONYMS: _____

   Other forms: _____

5. increase   The workers are asking for a 10-percent *increase* in pay.
   (INcrease)

   SYNONYMS: _____

   Other forms: _____

Field-specific   *For each of the following words, read the sentence and use the context to guess the definition. Write the meaning in your own words if possible.*

6. demographics   Generally, the *demographics* of a country are shown in a
   (demoGRAPHics)   census taken about every ten years.

   MEANING: _____

7. prime source   At home, your *prime source* for definitions of new words is
   (PRIME SOURCE)   your dictionary.

   MEANING: _____

8. sponsor   Companies and individuals often act as *sponsors* for students
   (SPONsor)   who go abroad.

   MEANING: _____

9. proportionately   *Proportionately*, I eat just as much meat as vegetables.
   (proPORtionately)

   MEANING: _____

E. Note-Taking Technique: Mapping

Traditionally, when people take notes during a lecture, they outline information in the order they hear it. As they are listening, they often take notes straight down the page. Another technique you can use is mapping. When you map your ideas, you draw lines to make connections between the different topics. This helps you to see the lecture as a whole. Some people also use this technique as a way to review material from class lectures or as a way to organize ideas for a composition.

Look at the following map. You will see one box in the center labeled *INTENSIVE ENGLISH CENTERS*. To one side is another box labeled *IN MAJOR U.S. UNIVERSITIES*. To the other side is a box labeled *TEACH ENGLISH*. Notice they are written in capital letters. As you listen to the paragraph that your teacher will read, look at the box and think about the way that mapping helps organize information in a different way.

14

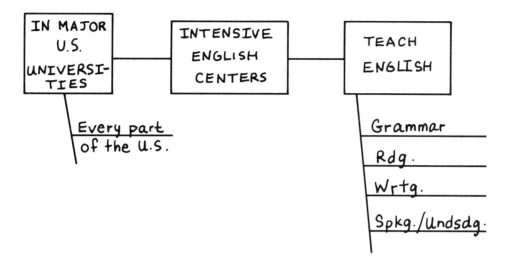

Fig. 2-1 Mapping practice

F. Main Idea/Organization Check

Read through these questions or statements before you listen to the tape. As you listen to the lecture for the first time, listen for the main ideas. Circle the letter of the best answer.

This is not a note-taking exercise. You will have a chance to take notes on the material later.

1. The lecturer explains _____ of foreign students.
   a. first the statistics on enrollment
   b. first the countries of origin
   c. only the current enrollment numbers

2. At the end of the lecture, Coan addresses _____.
   a. why students come to the United States
   b. how the number of students from each country is changing
   c. how the students feel after they have been in the United States for a short time

3. Coan gives many _____ about foreign students.
   a. statistics
   b. opinions
   c. anecdotes

4. Coan's lecture discusses _____.
   a. the jobs foreign students have in the United States
   b. foreign student numbers and countries of origin
   c. how to establish reliable statistics about foreign students

15

⊙⊙ G. Note-Taking Guide Page

Look at the note-taking outline on page 17. In the middle of the page, there are three boxes. In the center box, you can see the word *DEMOGRAPHICS*, which is the *main topic*. In the two boxes on the sides, you can see the subtopics *U.S. UNIVERSITIES* and *U.S. INTENSIVE ENG. PROGRAMS*. Notice these are written in capital letters.

On the lines connected to each subtopic are the *main points*: *A—TOTAL #*, *B—FIELDS OF STUDY*, *C—FUNDING*, and *E—OTHER FACTS*. These all refer to foreign students in U.S. universities. The only main point under Intensive English programs is *D—TOTAL #*. The lecturer will not say very much about this topic.

Connected to the main points are other lines. These horizontal lines are for *specific details*, such as numbers, names of countries, and names of specific fields.

As you listen to the lecture again, try to fill in the rest of the details in sections A, B, C, and D. The next time, fill in the facts for section E.

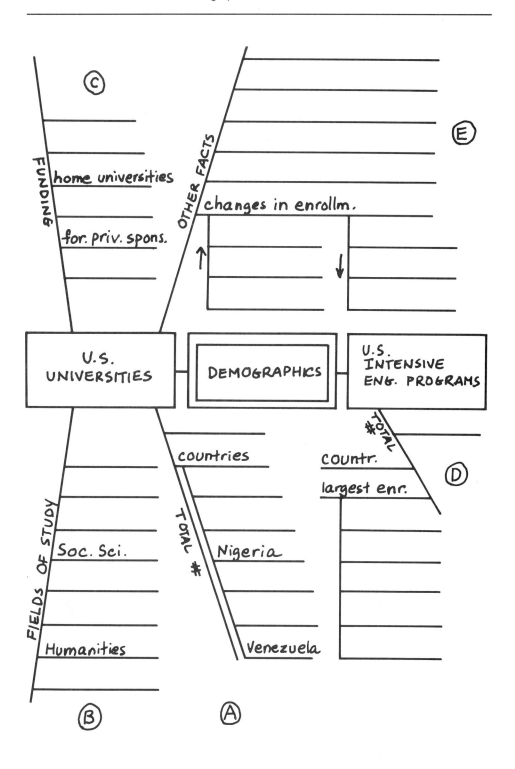

Fig. 2–2. Demographics of International Students

☐ From *Open Doors: 1984/85 Report on International Educational Exchange*, edited by Marianthi Zikopoulos, New York: Institute of International Education, 1985.

Lesson 2

H. Review Strategy: Mapping Generalizations

To help you remember the information in your notes, turn back to page 17, the note-taking guide page. Write a one paragraph summary of the important information on the map on a separate piece of paper.

I. Feature of the Lecture: Listing Signals

Coan uses phrases that tell the listener that a list of some kind will follow. Coan says, "It might be appropriate to give a little bit of information about . . . uh . . . fields of study . . ." This signals the listener that a list or additional information will follow.

Turn to the script for Coan on page 134 and follow the directions given.

J. Comprehension Exercise: True/False

Use your notes to decide whether each of the following statements is *true* or *false*. If the statement is *false*, underline the information that is incorrect. Change this information so that the statement will be true, according to the lecture. Circle *T* for true and *F* for false.

1. *T* *F*   There are about 242,000 foreign students studying in the United States.

2. *T* *F*   More students study business management than other fields.

3. *T* *F*   The primary source of student financial support is personal and family funding.

4. *T* *F*   Seventeen percent of the foreign students studying in the United States today are male.

5. *T* *F*   According to the lecture, in Intensive English programs, Nigeria is one of the countries that has shown an increase in the past few years.

6. *T* *F*   Almost 30 percent of all foreign students in the United States are not enrolled in four-year schools.

7. *T* *F*   Ten percent of all graduate students are foreign.

K. Comprehension Exercise: Short Essay

Choose one or two of the following topics. For each one, write a paragraph using information from your notes.

1. List the top three fields of study for foreign students in the United States. Briefly discuss why you think students choose these fields.
2. Discuss the countries of origin of students who attend U.S. universities.
3. Discuss the nationalities of students who are enrolled in U.S. Intensive English programs.

L. Discussion or Written Assignments

1. In your country, can you see any changes in the numbers and majors of students coming to the United States?

18

2. Why do you think the numbers of students go up for some countries and down for others? Give specific examples.

3. What do you think will happen in the future regarding numbers of foreign students in the United States?

4. Find a recent article with statistics about foreign students in the United States. Compare it with the information from the lecture. Report your findings to the class.

Discussion Notes

3/ Physiological Effects of Music

A. Speaker

Paul Haack is a professor of music education at the University of Minnesota. He has a doctorate from the University of Wisconsin at Madison. His teaching areas include the sociology and psychology of music, particularly as they relate to attitudes and values.

B. Background

This lecture is related to the field of music therapy. Music is used to change the moods of people to help them. Think of a favorite song and how it makes you feel. Then think of why it makes you feel that way.

C. Prelistening Discussion

1. Play some songs and discuss why you feel as you do when you listen to them.
2. Name different kinds of music (e.g., rock and roll, classical music) and tell how they affect you.

D. Prelistening Vocabulary

Before you listen to the lecture, practice the pronunciation of these key words with your teacher. Notice the syllable in each word with the most important stress.

General   *Read the sentence for each word. For* **synonyms***, think of another word or other words that could replace the italicized word. For* **other forms***, write in nouns, adjectives, or other word forms of the italicized word.*

1. sedative
   (SEDative)

   The book was like a *sedative*; it made me sleepy.

   SYNONYMS: _____ *calmative* _____

   Other forms: _____ *sedate, sedately, sedateness*

2. stimulate
   (STIMulate)

   The TV program on political issues *stimulated* a lot of discussion.

   SYNONYMS: _____

   Other forms: _____

3. energize
   (ENergize)

   The walk across campus will *energize* the students and help them study.

   SYNONYMS: _____

   Other forms: _____

4. melodies
   (MELodies)

   Melodies are the notes to the songs we sing.

   SYNONYMS: _____

   Other forms: _____

21

Field-specific   For each of the following words, read the sentence and use the context to guess the definition. Write the meaning in your own words.

5. harmonies
   (HARmonies)

   The *harmony* is the combination of notes into a chord.

   MEANING: _____

6. disjunct
   (disJUNCT)

   A *disjunct* melody is a jumpy one.

   MEANING: _____

7. dissonance
   (DISsonance)

   Dissonances occur in irregular harmonies.

   MEANING: _____

8. dynamics
   (dyNAMics)

   Changing *dynamics* can be stimulative.

   MEANING: _____

9. crescendos
   (creSCENdo)

   A *crescendo* is a gradual increase in sound.

   MEANING: _____

10. rhythms
    (RHYTHms)

    The *rhythm* is what makes us clap our hands to music.

    MEANING: _____

11. tempos
    (TEMpos)

    The *tempo* is one thing that makes rock music and waltzes different.

    MEANING: _____

E. Note-Taking Techniques: 1. Abbreviations
2. Parallel Headings

1. Abbreviations

To take good notes in college, you need to use some abbreviations to save time. The words that we usually abbreviate are ones that give information. Because every student takes notes differently, you need to decide which words you will abbreviate. A few examples of the ways people abbreviate are *temp.* for *temperature* and *incrsg* or ↗ for *increase*. On the note-taking page, notice the abbreviations already used. What do these abbreviations stand for? Write in your answers.

irreg. = *irregular*   const. = _____   melod. = _____

chng. = _____   rhyms. = _____   disj. = _____

harm. = _____   stimu. = _____   sedat. = _____

2. Parallel Headings

There are two common ways to take notes on topics that have two main divisions.

1. Separate headings: You can write the main idea or title of the lecture at the top of your note-taking page. Start with the first topic

mentioned and write notes down the page. Underline each main topic as it is written down.
See Example A below.

2. Side-by-side headings: The other common way to take notes is using a side-by-side heading. You can divide your note-taking page even further by making two columns. At the top of each column, you can place each main topic and underline it. Then add the details so that you can compare the two topics side-by-side. This is easier to do if your handwriting is small.
See Example B below.

After you have examined the two common ways to do this type of note-taking, try to complete the side-by-side heading form in Example B below.

Example A: *Two ways students react to test-taking*

Calm

Preparation
   Studies regularly
During tests
   Time — budgets time
   Confidence — keeps going
Attitude after test
   Doesn't worry

Nervous

Preparation
   Regular or last minute
During tests
   Time — doesn't budget time
   Confidence — worries a lot
Attitude after test
   Concerned about grade

Example B

Calm   *Nervous*

Preparation

◉◉ F. Main Idea/Organization Check

Read through these questions or statements before you listen to the tape. As you listen to the lecture for the first time, listen for the main ideas. Circle the letter of the best answer.

This is not a note-taking exercise. You will have a chance to take notes on the material later.

1. In the first few sentences, Haack talks about the two aspects of music. What are they?
   a. sedative-stimulative music
   b. stimulative-rock music
   c. sedative-disjunct music

2. Haack next explains the various ways _____.
   a. sedative music affects us
   b. stimulative music affects us
   c. only rock music can affect us

3. In the last section, Haack talks about music that makes us feel _____.
   a. relaxed
   b. excited
   c. bored

◉◉ G. Note-Taking Guide Page: Parallel Headings

Listen to the lecture and fill in the missing information about the lecture on page 25.

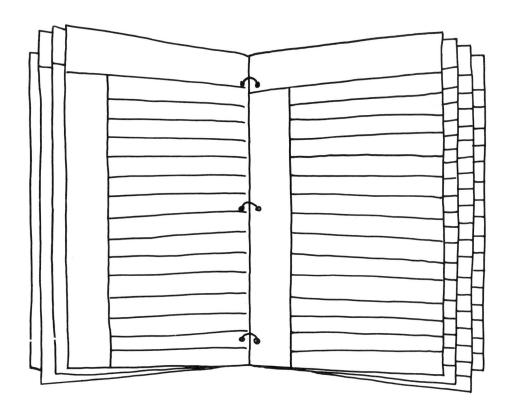

G. Note-Taking Guide Page

Main Topic: _Effects of Music_

Stimu.

Raises heart rate
Blood flow incr.

Blood pressure

incr. gal. skin resp.
Features of music
   disj. melod.
   irreg. rhyms.

What are two effects that music has on people?

_____

_____

_____

Sedat.

_____

Lower hrtbeat rate
Features of music
   smooth mel.

Name three things in music that stimulate us.

_____

_____

   const. tempos

_____

    Now organize the notes above in a side-by-side heading form as shown on page 23.

H. Review Strategy: Predicting Exam Questions

In the column to the left of the notes, you can see a question and a statement. These examples are similar to items you might see on a test. Look over the notes you have taken and write additional test items in the left-hand margin.

After you have made up the questions, you should cover the notes on the right with a blank piece of paper and ask yourself the questions. You can also ask a classmate to help you review. This will help you find out if you know the material or need to study it more before a test. If you do this weekly, it will also help you gradually review for midterms or final examinations that many teachers give.

I. Feature of the Lecture: Paraphrasing

One important feature of Haack's lecture is his use of paraphrasing for key words. For example, he says, "one of the ways it communicates or affects us seems . . ." He paraphrases, or gives another word for, key words. He does this by using the word *or* and a synonymn or similar phrase.

Turn to the script for Haack on page 136 and follow the directions given.

J. Comprehension Exercise: True/False

Use your notes to decide whether each of the following statements is *true* or *false*. If the statement is *false*, underline the information that is incorrect. Change this information so that the statement will be true, according to the lecture. Circle *T* for true and *F* for false.

1. *T*   *F*   The speaker says music can either stimulate or sedate us.

2. *T*   *F*   When we are stimulated, our heartbeats increase, our blood pressure decreases, and our galvanic skin response increases.

3. *T*   *F*   A synonym for stimulate is energize.

4. *T*   *F*   When we are sedated, our blood-flow rate rises.

5. *T*   *F*   Disjunct melodies are sedative.

6. *T*   *F*   An irregular harmony is one that doesn't flow as we anticipate.

7. *T*   *F*   Repeated rhythms are sedative.

8. *T*   *F*   The speaker would recommend rock and roll music for a nervous person.

9. *T*   *F*   The speaker says that the research findings on cross-cultural effects are conclusive.

K. Comprehension Exercise: Short Essay

Choose one of the following topics. Write a paragraph using information from your notes.

1. In a paragraph, summarize the features of stimulative and sedative music.
2. Using your two lists of characteristics, listen to two songs and then compare them. Were they stimulative or sedative? Why? Use your notes for reasons.

L. Discussion or Written Assignments

1. What kinds of music do you like? Why?

2. What music is popular in your country? Consider the music your parents like and what your friends like. Is some music popular only at special holidays?

3. How or where can music be used in industry and other situations?

4. Find an article about a concert in a magazine or newspaper, report to the class about the event, and tell if you think the music was stimulative or sedative.

5. Some people believe that governments should censor lyrics to some songs because they are too stimulative. Some of these lyrics contain violent or sexual material. Do you think these songs are a problem?

Discussion Notes

$$A = \frac{ab}{2}$$

$$C = \pi d$$

$$E = mc^2$$

$$D = \frac{M}{V}$$

$$A = \pi r^2$$

$$(F - 32)\,^5\!/_9 = C$$

LESSON
4 / An Electric Field

A. Speaker

Gordon G. Wiseman is a professor emeritus at the University of Kansas. His research is solid-state physics. Since 1943, he has taught physics courses at all levels. He has been a consultant for the U.S. Navy, Midwest Research Institute, Raven Industries, and Universidad de Oriente (Venezuela). He grew up and obtained his undergraduate education in South Dakota, so his accent and patterns of speech are characteristic of speakers from the Northern Plains States rather than from Kansas.

B. Background

In a physics lab, students are often required to measure quantities. The process for this is more complex than measuring liquids and solids because energy is involved.

C. Prelistening Discussion

Think about the work that takes place in a physics lab.

1. What types of phenomena do physicists study?
2. In your physics classes, what was the most interesting thing you learned?
3. Should everyone study physics?

D. Prelistening Vocabulary

Before you listen to the lecture, practice the pronunciation of the following key words with your teacher. Notice the syllable in each word with the most important stress.

General *Read the sentence for each word. For* **synonyms**, *think of another word or other words that could replace the italicized word. For* **other forms**, *write in nouns, adjectives, or other word forms of the italicized word.*

1. exerted
   (exERTed)

   He *exerted* pressure on his friends to stop drinking.

   SYNONYMS: ___*placed*___

   Other forms: ___*exertion*___

2. cautions
   (CAUtions)

   Before I started the job, one of the *cautions* the manager gave me was, "Always make a copy of every letter you send."

   SYNONYMS: _____

   Other forms: _____

3. shift
   (SHIFT)

   There will be a *shift* in the library hours during the summer session because there won't be as many students on campus.

   SYNONYMS: _____

   Other forms: _____

4. ratio
   (RAtio)

What is the *ratio* of men to women in executive positions in banking?

SYNONYMS: _____

Other forms: _____

5. source
   (SOURCE)

Before you publish that statistic, you should double-check the *source* of the information.

SYNONYMS: _____

Other forms: _____

Field-specific   *For each of the following words, read the sentence and use the context to guess the definition. Write the meaning in your own words if possible. Note that some of the following words are common in everyday language. It is important to recognize their technical meaning.*

6. operations
   (operAtions)

In order to find the answer, you must perform several separate *operations*.

MEANING: _____

7. electric field
   (eLECtric FIELD)

The space in the neighborhood of charged objects is called an *electric field*.

MEANING: _____

8. charge
   (CHARGE)

When you touch a desk or drawer after you walk on a carpet, you may feel a *charge* of electricity.

MEANING: _____

9. vector
   (VECtor)

A *vector* shows both magnitude and direction.

MEANING: _____

10. force
    (FORCE)

The object is exerting a downward *force* of ten pounds.

MEANING: _____

11. magnitude
    (MAGnitude)

The scientists wanted to know the *magnitude* of the explosion.

MEANING: _____

12. coulomb
    (COUlomb)

Physicists use *coulombs* to measure the amount of electric charge. One *coulomb* equals the amount of electric charge flowing through a 100-watt light bulb every second.

MEANING: _____

⊘⊘ **E. Main Idea/Organization Check**

Read through these questions or statements before you listen to the tape. As you listen to the lecture for the first time, listen for the main ideas. Circle the letter of the best answer.

This is not a note-taking exercise. You will have a chance to take notes on the material later.

1. Wiseman talks about how to _____ .
   a. measure a quantity
   b. pick an example
   c. define physics

2. The second part of Wiseman's explanation lists _____ .
   a. the operations to perform
   b. the type of charge to use
   c. types of forces

3. To give us the second part of the process, Wiseman says, _____ .
   a. "the second step would be"
   b. "the second . . . part . . . of the operation"
   c. "Secondly, you need to"

4. How many cautions does Wiseman mention?
   a. three
   b. two
   c. four

F. Note-Taking Technique: Indenting for Subtopics

It is important to make your notes as easy to read as possible. Sometimes you will look at them weeks after the class session and try to figure out what you wrote. In Lesson 1 you practiced using a formal outline. You learned how to separate main points and subtopics. If you indent, or leave about an inch before you begin your list of subtopics, you will locate information more quickly when you review.

In this lecture, listen for the process and the verbs that indicate the different steps. Use the indented lines to fill in the parts of this process.

⊙⊙

G. Note-Taking Guide Page

An Electric Field

Date _____

= _____

Quantities in physics —

OPERATIONS

    1. _____ a test charge q

    2. _____ F

    3. _____ $F = qE$

    _____

    F is a vector

_____

if large ⟶ _____ in the field

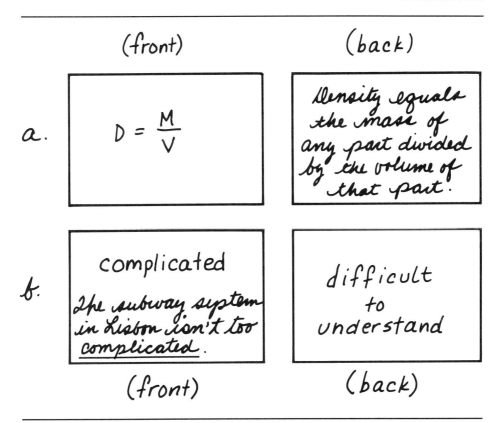

Fig. 4–1 Sample Notecards

H. Review Strategy: Memorizing from Notecards

Think of another concept or term that must be defined with an equation or formula. Explain this equation or formula to the class. See page 28 for some examples. What does each element in the formula represent?

1. _____

2. _____

3. _____

To help you memorize these formulas, you can make small cards with the formula on one side and the explanation on the other side. It's easier to use these cards if the paper is heavier than regular paper. That way you cannot see the answer on the other side.

You can keep these cards in your pocket, notebook, or backpack and review them when you have a few minutes between classes. You can review vocabulary or lists of facts with this system. As you study with the cards, divide them into two groups. When you get an answer correct, put the card into one pile. If you miss an answer, put the card into another pile. Then mix all the cards together again and go through the whole group.

⊘⊘ **I. Features of the Lecture:** **1. Stress on Key Words**
2. Use of Fillers

1. Stress on Key Words

In note-taking, we need to write key words that give us specific content information. Speakers generally put more emphasis on the nouns, verbs, adjectives, and adverbs when they explain an idea. You can hear the stressed word because it will sound louder and longer than other words. In one sentence, you may hear only a few key words.

Listen to your teacher read a few sentences. For each sentence, write just the key words you hear.

Ex. I'll pick you up at the bus station at five o'clock. *pick up - bus - five*

1. _____

2. _____

3. _____

2. Use of Fillers

When lecturers speak to students, they can read from notes or speak more informally. When they do not read complete sentences, they often need to think a little before going on to the next point in the explanation. When native speakers of English hesitate, they often fill the time with the sound *uh*. Another way to fill in the time is to say *um*, *or*, and *like*. Have you heard these fillers? What sounds or words do speakers of other languages use as fillers?

Turn to the script for Wiseman on page 137 and follow the directions given.

J. Comprehension Exercise: True/False

Use your notes to decide whether each of the following statements is *true* or *false*. If the statement is *false*, underline the information that is incorrect. Change this information so that the statement will be true, according to the lecture. Circle *T* for true and *F* for false.

1. *T* *F* The definition of an electric field is a ratio.

2. *T* *F* We use *t* to represent the test charge.

3. *T* *F* We use *F* to measure the size of the field.

4. *T* *F* A vector has direction and magnitude.

5. *T* *F* A large test charge will cause very little shift in the source of the electric field.

K. Comprehension Exercise: Short Essay

Choose one of the following topics. Write a paragraph using information from your notes.

1. List the operations required to measure an electric field.
2. Describe the type of test charge you should use in this process. Why is it important to use this type of charge?

L. Discussion or Written Assignments

1. Make a set of 20 small notecards to help you review formulas or vocabulary words. Put the word or formula on one side and the definition or explanation on the other side. Study these for a few days, and then you will take a short quiz on the words or formulas you studied.

2. Conduct a simple experiment to measure a quantity. What could you measure? Consider volume, electricity, pressure, or velocity. Work in groups of three or four. What materials would you need to measure the quantity? Think of something you could do in the classroom with simple materials you could bring from home. Measure the quantity. Then when you finish, write down each step that you followed. Did anything surprise you? What cautions can you think of? Write your notes clearly so that another person could repeat your experiment.

3. In which fields is a solid knowledge of physics more essential? (aerospace, history, music, electrical engineering, architecture, medicine)

4. In a magazine or newspaper, find an article about some recent research in physics, and report on it to the class.

Discussion Notes

LESSON
5/ Tji Wara: A Headcrest Mask

A. Speaker

Robert T. Soppelsa is an associate professor of art history at Washburn University in Topeka, Kansas. He has a doctorate in art history from Ohio State University. Since 1972, he has specialized in the study of African art. Soppelsa lived in the Ivory Coast for three years. He has served as a consultant on African art collections in midwestern universities.

B. Background

We can learn a great deal about a culture's history and social activities from art objects that we can find in museums. Sometimes, however, it is difficult to understand the importance of an art object unless we know more about its cultural setting.

For example, in the United States, women in primarily rural areas used to get together to make a special type of blanket called a quilt. They would make these quilts as gifts for weddings, births, or other special occasions. Making these quilts also gave women an opportunity to socialize and work together.

C. Prelistening Discussion

In this lecture, you will hear about a mask used in a traditional masquerade in an agricultural society.

1. What is a masquerade?
2. Are you familiar with any celebrations that involve people wearing costumes?
3. Why do they wear such costumes?

D. Prelistening Vocabulary

Before you listen to the lecture, practice the pronunciation of the following key words with your teacher. Notice the syllable in each word with the most important stress.

General   *Read the sentence for each word. For* **synonyms,** *think of another word or other words that could replace the italicized word. For* **other forms,** *write in nouns, adjectives, or other word forms of the italicized word.*

1. mask
   (MASK)

   For Halloween, the boy wore a *mask* that looked like Dracula.

   SYNONYMS: *costume (face), disguise*

   Other forms: *masking tape*

2. cultivate
   (CULtivate)

   Farmers are trying to *cultivate* better types of grains.

   SYNONYMS: _____

   Other forms: _____

3. elegant
   (ELegant)

   The couple looked very *elegant* in their formal clothes.

   SYNONYMS: _____

   Other forms: _____

37

4. role
(ROLE)

A college adviser can play an important *role* in a student's academic career.

SYNONYMS: _____

Other forms: _____

5. harvest
(HARvest)

At *harvest* time, farmers can measure the yield of their crops for the season.

SYNONYMS: _____

Other forms: _____

6. context
(CONtext)

When you see an unfamiliar word in your reading, try to use the *context* of the sentence or paragraph to help you guess the meaning.

SYNONYMS: _____

Other forms: _____

Field-specific   *For each of the following words, read the sentence and use the context to guess the definition. Write the meaning in your own words if possible.*

7. masquerade
(masqueRADE)

In Rio de Janeiro, Brazil, there is a famous *masquerade* to celebrate Mardi Gras.

MEANING: _____

8. myth
(MYTH)

Many people believe in *myths* and legends, although they have no concrete evidence for them.

MEANING: _____

9. antelope
(ANTelope)

An *antelope* is a swift animal with horns that looks somewhat like a deer.

MEANING: _____

10. anthropomorphically
(anthropoMORphically)

In art or architecture, when animals are represented *anthropomorphically*, their heads appear human and they sometimes wear clothes or jewelry.

MEANING: _____

11. carved
(CARVED)

The old man started with a piece of wood and ended up with a beautifully *carved* figure of a fisherman.

MEANING: _____

12. mane
    (MANE)

The man brushed the horse's *mane* while the horse lowered its head.

MEANING: _____

E. Note-Taking Technique: 1. Writing Preview Questions

Look at the picture of the headcrest on page 42 and refer again to the title of this lecture. Think of three questions that you think the lecturer might answer. If you listen for the answers to these questions while the professor is talking, you will be a more active listener and you will be able to hear more information for your notes.

Ex. What does *tji wara* mean?
      Who wore this headcrest mask?

Write your three questions at the top of page 43. As the lecturer speaks, listen for the answers to your questions.

F. Main Idea/Organization Check

Read through these questions or statements before you listen to the tape. As you listen to the lecture for the first time, listen for the main ideas. Circle the letter of the best answer.

This is not a note-taking exercise. You will have a chance to take notes on the material later.

1. What complex art form does Soppelsa explain at the beginning of his lecture?
   a. sculpture
   b. dancing
   c. masquerade

2. What do the words *tji wara* mean in Bamana?
   a. costumed dancer
   b. cultivator beast
   c. mother and baby

3. What two figures does this mask represent?
   a. a mother and father antelope
   b. a mother and baby antelope
   c. a human mother and an antelope

4. What does the next part of the lecture explain?
   a. the features of the antelopes
   b. the movements of the dancers
   c. the divisions of the society

5. What is another meaning for *tji wara*?
   a. a celebration of life
   b. a special initiation
   c. a young men's organization

6. The masquerade takes place _____.
   a. only for harvests
   b. for important events
   c. for the older people

G. Note-Taking Technique: 2. Leaving Space for Details

Some lecturers give a lot of information, or a series of points, very quickly. When you hear phrases such as *there are several kinds . . .* , *three things to . . .* , *one of the . . .* , you know that the lecturer will give more than one point. It is not always possible to write down all of this information at once. A lecturer will often return to the main points later in the lecture and clarify them or give more specific examples. If you leave some blank spaces as you take notes, you can go back later and complete the information.

Early in this lecture, listen for a series of points. The lecturer will say, "*a very complex art form involving . . .*" Later, the lecturer will say, "*As I said, . . .*" and he will return to these same points. Go back to the beginning of your notes and fill in the details.

There are many ways to indicate a list or series of ideas in your notes. Which way do you think is the best for you?

1. **numbering**

   EFFECTS OF THE NEW GOVERNMENT
   1. cultural
   2. political
   3. historical

2. **brackets**

   PLACES TO USE COMPUTERS
   { home   [home
     school   school
     work   work

3. **indenting for a list or**
   drawing arrows to the main point

   NEW SYSTEM OF
   CHECKING
   Disadvantages
      high cost
      time

4. **diagonal lines extending**
   from the topic

   HOW ANTELOPES–REPRESENTED

   male   female

5. **a mark next to each detail**

   APPEARANCE
   –elegant   • elegant
   –tall   • tall
   –graceful   • graceful

Your teacher will give you some information about a popular artist or singer. You will hear information about different aspects of this person's life. Write a heading for these subtopics. Listen for the lists of examples. In the following space, write down each list and make sure you can distinguish each item.

_____

_____

_____

_____

Mali Republic, Africa, Bambara tribe, Female antelope figure, wood, brass tacks, string, cowrie shells, iron, quills, height: 85.5 cm, Ada Turnbull Hertle Fund, 1965.7 © 1988 The Art Institute of Chicago. All Rights Reserved.

42

⊙⊙

H. Note-Taking Guide Page

Date: _____

Preview Questions

Ex. *What does tji wara mean?*

Ex. *Who wore this headcrest mask?*

1.
2.
3.
_____

TJI WARA = _____

from Mali, _____ Africa

Mask ⟵ masquerade

an _____ work of art

ELEMENTS OF MASQUERADE
1.
2. song
3.
4.
5.
6. audience
7.

ANTELOPE = _____ beast

1. Bamana myth —

   antelope taught _____

2. Mask — like human

   a. mother — elegant, _____

   b. _____ baby — complex mane
      _____

3. Dance — in pairs

1 _____ and 1 _____ — like society

TJI WARA = _____ organization

   ages _____

   prepares men for _____

WHY DANCES ARE IMPORTANT
1. occasions — _____ , _____

2. notions of _____

43

I. Review Strategy: Answering Preview Questions

When you finish listening to the lecture, go back and see if you can answer your preview questions using your notes. If you can't answer them all, check with a classmate. Your notes may contain different information. If the lecturer did not answer your questions, make a guess from your notes or your own knowledge. During a class, you might have the chance to ask these questions. Sometimes, one lecture covers only a few aspects of a topic. Lecturers often continue discussing a topic for several days or they may require you to get the rest of the information from your text or other sources.

J. Feature of the Lecture: Emphatic Pauses After Key Words

In his lecture, Soppelsa uses pauses to emphasize key words. He often pauses just after an important term or fact. This gives you, the listener, time to write down the key word. As you listen to the lecture again, notice how he repeats and summarizes important details in the last sections of the lecture.

Turn to the script for Soppelsa on page 138 and follow the directions given.

K. Comprehension Exercise: True/False

Use your notes to decide whether each of the following statements is *true* or *false*. If the statement is *false*, underline the information that is incorrect. Change this information so that the statement will be true, according to the lecture. Circle *T* for true and *F* for false.

1. *T* *F* A *tji wara*, or headcrest mask, is a complete art form.

2. *T* *F* The song and location of the dance are also important.

3. *T* *F* In the Bamana language, *tji wara* means harvest.

4. *T* *F* In some masks, antelopes are given human-like features.

5. *T* *F* There is less detail on the male antelope in this mask.

6. *T* *F* Tji wara also refers to a family organization.

7. *T* *F* The people in the organization range in age from 8 to 40.

8. *T* *F* Some of the dances are done at harvest time.

9. *T* *F* The audience and the dancers interact.

10. *T* *F* The dances are mainly done to remind people of their childhood.

L. Comprehension Exercise: Short Essay

Choose one or two of the following topics. For each one, write a paragraph using information from your notes.

1. What elements are important in a masquerade?
2. In Bamana folklore, what is the importance of the antelope?
3. Briefly describe the way the Bamana dance wearing the tji wara.
4. List several occasions when these dances are performed.

M. Discussion or Written Assignments

1. Do you know about other special ceremonies for young adult men and women?

2. Think of an object that represents a larger event in your own culture. Is there a ceremony involved? Is this ceremony still popular today? with whom?

3. How do you feel when you look at art in a museum? What type of art do you prefer to look at in museums? Why do some people find museums boring? fascinating? educational?

4. Do you know any stories about animals that look or act like humans? Share one of these stories with some of your classmates.

5. In an art history or anthropology magazine or encyclopedia, read more about an art form that is very dynamic. Think about the setting and ceremony involved. Make a short report to the class.

Discussion Notes

A. Speaker

Philip Montgomery is an associate professor of mathematics at the University of Kansas. He holds a doctorate from Washington University in St. Louis, Missouri. His research areas include algebra and group theory. Montgomery is the coordinator of all freshman and sophomore algebra and calculus courses at the University of Kansas.

B. Background

Mathematics involves many abstract concepts that help describe the real world. People in the business world use mathematical formulas to predict the profits on their products and services. Scientists also use math to analyze natural phenomena such as motion, gravity, and population growth.

C. Prelistening Discussion

Discuss these questions with your teacher and classmates before listening to the lecture.

1. What was the last math class you took?
2. How do you use math in your daily life?
3. How are the notes you take for a math class similar to or different from notes for other classes?

D. Prelistening Vocabulary

Before you listen to the lecture, practice the pronunciation of the following key words with your teacher. Notice the syllable in each word with the most important stress.

General   *Read the sentence for each word. For **synonyms**, think of another word or other words that could replace the italicized word. For **other forms**, write in nouns, adjectives, or other word forms of the italicized word.*

1. steepness
   (STEEPness)

   The *steepness* of the hill made the climb difficult.

   SYNONYMS: _____ *incline* _____

   Other forms: _____ *steep* _____

2. horizontal
   (horiZONTal)

   We sleep in a *horizontal* position.

   SYNONYMS: _____

   Other forms: _____

3. vertical
   (VERtical)

   The ladder was almost *vertical* to the ground so that the fireman could climb up to the window.

   SYNONYMS: _____

   Other forms: _____

47

Lesson 6

4. indication
   (indiCAtion)

This hard work is an *indication* of his sincere attitude.

SYNONYMS: _____

Other forms: _____

5. obtained
   (obTAINED)

The student *obtained* his grade for the course yesterday.

SYNONYMS: _____

Other forms: _____

Field-specific *For each of the following words, read the sentence and use the information to help you draw an illustration of the concept.*

6. slope
   (SLOPE)

The *slope* of a line is the measure of an angle from a level direction.

ILLUSTRATION:

7. hypotenuse
   (hyPOTenuse)

The *hypotenuse* is the side of a right triangle opposite the right angle.

ILLUSTRATION:

8. line segment
   (LINE SEGment)

A *line segment* is the section of a line between two points.

ILLUSTRATION:

E. Note-Taking Technique: Labeling a Diagram

When students take notes in a mathematics class, they usually write down a formula that is explained. They will not take the outline or mapping kind of notes that have been explained in other lessons. If they write any kind of formal notes, the notes will be an explanation of when the formula is used. The notes will not be long and will follow the diagram that they have copied from the chalkboard or overhead projector.

Directions

1. See the next page for the actual note-taking diagram.
2. Notice the blanks near parts of the diagram. On the left is a list of terms. As you listen to the tape, fill in the correct label for each part.
3. After you label the diagram, check your answers with the teacher or another student.

F. Note-Taking Guide Page

Topic: _Slope of a Line_

rise
M
R
length
hypotenuse
run
height
right angle
triangle

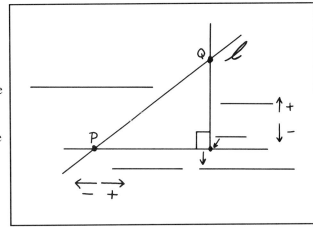

Fig. 6–1 Labeling a Diagram

Listen to the tape again. This time, as you follow Montgomery's explanation, draw the diagram for yourself. Make sure you label all the parts. In a math class, you often need to copy a diagram from the board into your notes.

G. Review Strategy: Practice with Diagrams

To check your understanding of the slope of a line, you could quiz yourself with practice diagrams. Which picture best represents each value for the slope of the line? Write the answers below each graph.
(0, −1, 1/2, +2, no slope)

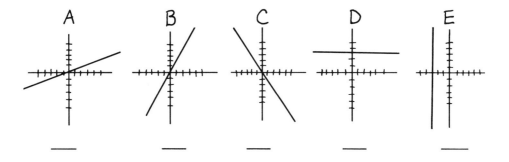

Fig. 6–2 Diagram Practice

⊙⊙ **H. Features of the Lecture:** 1. **Focus Cues**
                                      2. **Contrastive Stress**

1. Focus Cues

In the first part of Montgomery's explanation, he wants you to draw and label a diagram. To help you do this, he gives certain focus cues such as . . . *in the following way* . . . , *now* . . . , and *you should then have.* . . . He also uses *this* and *that* to represent certain line segments.

2. Contrastive Stress

The second half of the lecture gives generalizations about the slope of various kinds of lines. Montgomery stresses adjectives and adverbs such as *horizontal*, *vertical*, *positively*, and *negatively* to show contrast in the measurement of slope. Look for expressions that are exactly opposite in meaning and listen for the stress and intonation of those phrases.

Turn to the script for Montgomery on page 141 and follow the directions given.

I. Comprehension Exercise: True/False

Use your notes to decide whether each of the following statements is *true* or *false*. If the statement is *false*, underline the information that is incorrect. Change this information so that the statement will be true, according to the lecture. Circle *T* for true and *F* for false.

1. *T*   *F*   A slope indicates the steepness of a line.

2. *T*   *F*   In order to find the slope you must pick three points on the line.

3. *T*   *F*   The line segment across from the right angle of the triangle is called the rise.

4. *T*   *F*   For horizontal lines, if you measure the distance from left to right, the sign will be positive.

5. *T*   *F*   The slope of a telephone pole is 0.

6. *T*   *F*   A flat table has no slope.

J. Discussion or Written Assignments

1. Choose three or four graphs from a newspaper or news magazine. What does each of the graphs represent? What do the different slopes of the lines represent?

2. Do you think that students in other countries are better prepared in mathematics than those in the United States? Why or why not?

3. Some studies have shown that men usually score higher than women on math tests. Do you agree that this is true?

4. Does a person's success in mathematics affect his or her choice of a career? Give several examples.

Adjustment of Students
(Part A)

A. Speaker

Diane McDermott is an associate professor of counseling psychology at the University of Kansas. She received her doctorate in counseling from the University of Wisconsin in 1970 and has been both teaching and practicing counseling at Kansas since 1972. Her specialty areas are drug-abuse and alcohol counseling and research and cross-cultural issues related to chemical dependency. She also counsels students on a wide variety of concerns in her capacity as Counselor at the University Counseling Center.

B. Background

In the United States, students at the age of 17 or 18 many times go to another town or another state to begin university studies. Although this helps prepare the students for life by themselves, they will sometimes have difficulty adjusting to being away from home.

In the United States, children are expected to establish an independent life after they complete their education. The American idea of extended family only means a continued emotional closeness to their families throughout life. It does not mean that the children will live in the same house or even in the same part of the country after they are adults.

University students will many times attend schools very far away from home. Because they will live in group housing units such as dormitories, scholarship halls, or social organizations, they may have difficulty adjusting to university life. They may go to a counseling center to talk with a counselor about their adjustment to the new situation.

C. Prelistening Discussion

1. What adjustment problems do students have?
2. Where do students from your city live if they attend a university?

D. Prelistening Vocabulary

Before you listen to the lecture, practice the pronunciation of the following key words with your teacher. Notice the syllable in each word with the most important stress.

*General   Read the sentence for each word. For **synonyms**, think of another word or other words that could replace the italicized word. For **other forms**, write in nouns, adjectives, or other word forms of the italicized word.*

1. developmental
   (developMENTal)

   A child passes through many *developmental* stages on the way to maturity.

   SYNONYMS: _growth, maturation_

   Other forms: _development, developmentally_

2. identity
   (iDENTity)

   For many people, their job is their *identity*.

   SYNONYMS: _____

   Other forms: _____

53

Lesson 7

3. differential
   (diffeRENtial)

   The *differential* feature between the twin girls was their hair color.

   SYNONYMS: _____

   Other forms: _____

4. siblings
   (SIBlings)

   The two *siblings* in the family were always fighting.

   SYNONYMS: _____

   Other forms: _____

5. options
   (OPtions)

   In the cafeteria, a person has many dessert *options* to choose from.

   SYNONYMS: _____

   Other forms: _____

6. apartments
   (aPARTments)

   Many university students live in *apartments* and cook their own food.

   SYNONYMS: _____

   Other forms: _____

7. residence halls
   (RESidence HALLS)

   In a *residence hall*, the students eat in a cafeteria together.

   SYNONYMS: _____

   Other forms: _____

8. scholarship halls
   (SCHOlarship HALLS)

   A student must have good grades to live in a *scholarship hall*.

   SYNONYMS: _____

   Other forms: _____

9. overwhelming
   (overWHELMing)

   Homework is sometimes *overwhelming* to students if they are not used to reading several hours a day.

   SYNONYMS: _____

   Other forms: _____

10. overseeing
    (overSEEing)

    The *overseeing* of students is done by professors.

    SYNONYMS: _____

    Other forms: _____

54

Idioms   Read the following paragraph. Try to guess the meaning of the <u>underlined</u> phrases, and write the meaning in the spaces provided.

Some boys met outside the school. There was a disagreement between two of them. <u>Right off the bat</u>, one of the two tried to hit the other. The second boy tried to <u>break away</u> from the group and go home but could not because of the crowd. Mr. Smith, the principal, saw the trouble outside the school and knew that he <u>had to deal with</u> the disturbance. It was his responsibility.

11. break away
    (BREAK aWAY)   MEANING: _____

12. right off the bat
    (RIGHT OFF THE BAT)   MEANING: _____

13. have to deal with
    (HAVE TO DEAL WITH) MEANING: _____

Now rewrite the paragraph in standard English in the space provided.

_____

_____

_____

_____

_____

⊙⊙ E. Main Idea/Detail Check

Read through these questions or statements before you listen to the tape. As you listen to the lecture for the first time, listen for the main ideas as well as details. Circle the letter of the best answer.

This is not a note-taking exercise. You will have a chance to take notes on the material later.

1. In the beginning of the lecture, McDermott explains that she sees 5 to 10 people each week with student _____ problems.
   a. academic
   b. adjustment
   c. discipline

2. One of the main problems that students face is having too many different _____ .
   a. decisions
   b. needs
   c. clothes

3. Letter _____ of the following choices is *not* mentioned in the lecture.
   a. residence halls
   b. apartments
   c. private housing

55

F. Comprehension Exercise: Short Essay

Choose one of the following topics. Write a paragraph using information from your notes.

1. McDermott mentioned several adjustments of university students. What are some of the most common ones?
2. Consider one of the adjustments mentioned. Compare it with one for students you know. Explain how the situation is the same or different.

Discussion Notes

8/ Adjustment of Students (Part B)

A. Speaker

Turn to page 53 in Lesson 7.

B. Background

This section of the lecture considers some of the major decisions that university students must make on their own because they are away from home. The young students must decide when to study or how to handle the alcohol and drugs that they may encounter. Many students go to a counselor to decide how to cope with these and other decisions that come with their new environment.

C. Prelistening Discussion

1. What kinds of decisions do young university students have to make?
2. When students in your country need advice on how to cope with a problem, who can help them?

D. Prelistening Vocabulary

Before you listen to the lecture, practice the pronunciation of the following key words with your teacher. Notice the syllable in each word with the most important stress.

General   *Read the sentence for each word. For **synonyms**, think of another word or other words that could replace the italicized word. For **other forms**, write in nouns, adjectives, or other word forms of the italicized word.*

1. requirement
   (reQUIREment)

   It is a *requirement* that students do their homework every day.

   SYNONYMS: *demand, obligation*

   Other forms: *require, prerequisite*

2. flunking
   (FLUNKing)

   When a student is *flunking* a course, he or she may have to take it again the next semester.

   SYNONYMS: _____

   Other forms: _____

3. midterm
   (MIDterm)

   The *midterm* exams are given halfway through the semester.

   SYNONYMS: _____

   Other forms: _____

4. illegal
   (ilLEgal)

   In some countries, it is *illegal* to use cocaine and other dangerous drugs.

   SYNONYMS: _____

   Other forms: _____

5. pressure
   (PRESsure)

   Students experience a lot of *pressure* just before an exam.

   SYNONYMS: _____

   Other forms: _____

6. sheltered
   (SHELtered)

   Young children often lead very *sheltered* lives.

   SYNONYMS: _____

   Other forms: _____

7. maturity
   (maTURity)

   A student can be mentally mature, but not have reached emotional *maturity*.

   SYNONYMS: _____

   Other forms: _____

Idioms   Read the following paragraph. Try to guess the meaning of the underlined *phrases, and write the meaning in the space provided.*

Mark was walking home one day when he saw one of his friends, Bob, just ahead of him. He tried to catch up to his friend, but he could not. Suddenly, Mark's girlfriend, Ellen, joined Bob and kissed him. When Mark saw that, he looked very upset, but quite frankly, later he just blew it off. The fact of the matter is that Mark had planned to stop seeing Ellen and this gave him an excuse. Because Ellen now had a new boyfriend, Mark would not have to deal with mopping up a difficult situation.

8. catch up to
   (CATCH UP to)   MEANING: _____

9. quite frankly
   (QUITE FRANKly)   MEANING: _____

10. blow it off
    (BLOW IT OFF)   MEANING: _____

11. the fact of the matter is
    (THE FACT OF THE MATter IS)   MEANING: _____

12. mopping up
    (MOPping UP)   MEANING: _____

Now rewrite the paragraph in standard English in the space provided.

_____

_____

_____

_____

_____

E. Note-Taking Techniques: 1. Standard Outline
2. Personal Examples

1. Standard Outline

Listen to the paragraph that your teacher will read about starting elementary school. Take notes in the following space, and on a separate piece of paper try to organize them in a standard outline form.

2. Personal Examples

As we listen to lectures, we make connections with our own lives. This is a necessary part of active listening. If we try to apply the concept to a situation we know, we can better understand and remember the professor's explanation. Look at the outline on elementary school and try to add personal examples from your life to the left of the outline. That will help you remember what your teacher has read to you.

_____

_____

_____

_____

_____

_____

_____

_____

_____

F. Main Idea/Organization Check

Read through these questions or statements before you listen to the tape. As you listen to the lecture for the first time, listen for the main ideas. Circle the letter of the best answer.

This is not a note-taking exercise. You will have a chance to take notes on the material later.

1. According to the lecture, many freshmen especially have trouble around _____
   _____ .
   a. holidays
   b. midterms
   c. finals

2. According to the lecture, students who get into trouble with drugs or alcohol are many times _____ .
   a. sheltered or not mature enough to cope
   b. sheltered and reject those temptations
   c. having trouble dealing with reality

3. McDermott suggests that students should go to counselors to _____.
   a. straighten out problems
   b. confuse them
   c. help prevent problems

⊙⊙ G. Note-Taking Guide Page

As you listen to the tape for Lessons 7 and 8, try to fill in the missing information on the outline on page 63.

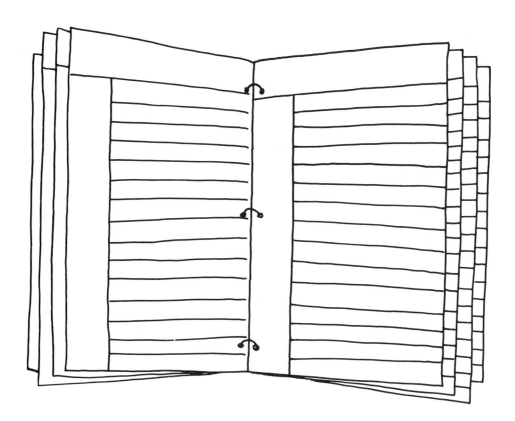

G. Note-Taking Guide Page

I. Student Adjustment Problems

    A. Reasons

        1. *Going through self-identity process*

        2. _____

    B. Decisions

        1. _____

        2. _____

    C. Responsibilities

        1. _____

        2. Health habits

        3. _____

        4. Going to class

        5. _____

    D. Personal choices

        1. Peer pressure

            a. _____

        2. Sex

II. Going for Help

    A. Good as a preventive measure

H. Review Strategy: Making Notes on the Left Side of the Margin

Look at the outline you made on page 63 and add personal examples to the left side of the margin that will help you remember what McDermott said.

I. Feature of the Lecture: Signal Phrases

When people talk, they use phrases or words that signal to the listener that they are beginning a new topic. Some examples are *and*, *another thing*, *to begin with*, and *one of the*.

Turn to the scripts for McDermott Parts A and B on page 143 and page 145 and follow the directions given.

J. Comprehension Exercise: Short Essay

Choose one of the following topics. Write a paragraph using information from your notes.

1. According to McDermott, what major problems do students usually have when they begin college?
2. What does the lecturer recommend when a student has important decisions to make?

K. Discussion or Written Assignments

1. How is university life different in different places?
2. Do students try to establish an independence from their families in your country or is the extended family valued more? Use a personal story to illustrate your point.
3. What kind of shared living space do students in your country experience?
4. When students must share their living space, what kind of rules should they establish about noise in the living space? Who should decide when or if friends can come to visit?
5. McDermott talked about adjustments of undergraduate students. What kinds of adjustments do married students or graduate students have to make when they go to another country to study?
6. Are there some universal adjustments that all people must make?
7. Interview a foreign student who has lived in this country for a long time. Report to the class what that student thinks was the major adjustment problem he or she had.

Discussion Notes

A. Speaker

Lawrence L. Brady is an associate scientist in the Geologic Investigations Section of the Kansas Geological Survey at the University of Kansas. He has a doctorate in geology from Kansas, and his area of research is mainly in coal geology and coal resources. Other areas of interest include economic mineral deposits and petroleum geology of Kansas. Prior to his present position at the Kansas Geological Survey, Brady was an assistant professor of geology at Oklahoma State University and also worked as an engineering geologist for the U.S. Army Corps of Engineers in the Kansas City District.

B. Background

The cost of gas and other petroleum products affects our lives. This lecture covers petroleum and its connection to geology. Petroleum is formed underground, and this speaker will help you understand how and why this happens.

C. Prelistening Discussion

Read these questions and then read the following section from the lecture. Answer the questions in a word or two.

1. How many factors are there that affect petroleum formation?
2. What is the name of the place underground where oil collects?
3. What is the name of the rock where the material to form oil originates?

> Today I wanna talk about petroleum and geology. There are five important factors when we think about the occurrence and why we have petroleum. There's source rock which is the rock in which the organic material or petroleum is actually derived, the reservoir rock which by the process of migration carries the uh . . . oil from the source rock to another mechanism called the trap. The trap then is where the petroleum accumulates and where we presently would obtain by oil wells the material. Within that trap, though, in order to contain the petroleum we have what we call the seal.

D. Prelistening Vocabulary

Before you listen to the lecture, practice the pronunciation of the following key words with your teacher. Notice the syllable in each word with the most important stress.

General *Read the sentence for each word. For* **synonyms**, *think of another word or other words that could replace the italicized word. For* **other forms**, *write in nouns, adjectives, or other word forms of the italicized word.*

1. mechanism (MECHanism)

The *mechanism* that makes a car move involves the engine, wheels, and other important parts.

SYNONYMS: *tool, apparatus*

Other forms: *mechanistic, mechanistically*

2. accumulate
   (acCUmulate)

Students *accumulate* many books before they graduate.

SYNONYMS: _____

Other forms: _____

3. composed
   (comPOSED)

Some desserts are *composed* mostly of sugar.

SYNONYMS: _____

Other forms: _____

4. derived
   (deRIVED)

Butter is *derived* from milk.

SYNONYMS: _____

Other forms: _____

5. squeezed
   (SQUEEZED)

When the boy was frightened, he *squeezed* his mother's hand.

SYNONYMS: _____

Other forms: _____

6. migrates
   (MIgrates)

The monarch butterfly *migrates* to Mexico every winter.

SYNONYMS: _____

Other forms: _____

7. encounter
   (enCOUNter)

When a person walks in the country, he may *encounter* many animals.

SYNONYMS: _____

Other forms: _____

8. approximate
   (apPROXimate)

The boy's *approximate* height was six feet.

SYNONYMS: _____

Other forms: _____

9. bend
   (BEND)

The girl *bends* over and ties her shoes.

SYNONYMS: _____

Other forms: _____

10. porous
    (POrous)

That material is *porous*; the water comes through easily.

SYNONYMS: _____

Other forms: _____

11. buoyancy
    (BUOYancy)

The woman had good *buoyancy*; she could float easily in the water.

SYNONYMS: _____

Other forms: _____

Field-specific   *In this mini-lecture, Brady defines many of the field-specific vocabulary words. Read the following sentences aloud to help you recognize these terms when you listen to the lecture.*

12. source rock
    (SOURCE ROCK)

A *source rock* is where petroleum is made.

13. organic rock
    (orGANic ROCK)

Petroleum is formed from *organic rock* by heat and pressure.

14. trap
    (TRAP)

A *trap* is where oil collects.

15. seal
    (SEAL)

A *seal* keeps oil from escaping.

16. marine derived
    (maRINE deRIVED)

The source rock is many times *marine derived*.

17. anticline
    (ANticline)

An *anticline* helps keep the oil in one place.

18. dome
    (DOME)

A *dome* forms a trap to let the oil gather in one place.

19. stratigraphic trap
    (stratiGRAPHic TRAP)

An example of a *stratigraphic trap* is an ancient sandstone river.

E. Note-Taking Technique: Labeling a Diagram

In the field of geology it is often necessary to use diagrams to explain how the earth is formed and what it looks like. A good way to take notes on this kind of lecture is to draw a picture of what the lecturer describes and then label the parts of the diagram. Many times the lecturer will draw a picture like the following one and give students some time to not only label the parts but also list the key words and

69

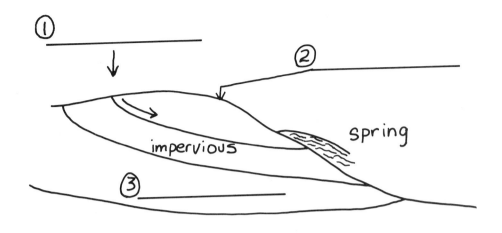

Fig. 9-1 A Spring
(where someone can get drinking water)

their meanings below the diagram. Listen to your teacher read a short paragraph about a spring and try to fill in the missing words in the diagram. If you have time, list some of the important words in the spaces following the diagram, and guess their meaning.

_____

_____

_____

_____

⊙⊙ F. Main Idea/Organization Check

Read through these questions or statements before you listen to the tape. As you listen to the lecture for the first time, listen for the main ideas. Circle the letter of the best answer.

This is not a note-taking exercise. You will have a chance to take notes on the material later.

1. There are _____ important factors that help form petroleum.
    a. three
    b. five
    c. four

2. The lecture _____.
    a. gives one basic term
    b. gives terms and defines them
    c. gives explanations and paraphrases them

3. Brady explains _____.
    a. the factors in petroleum formation
    b. the changes in world oil prices
    c. the problems with using oil for fuel

4. Brady explains the difference between _____.
    a. gas and other fuels
    b. a dome and an anticline
    c. source rock and petroleum

G. Note-Taking Guide Page: Labeling a Diagram

Turn to page 72 and listen to the tape. At the top of the page is Figure 9–2, which is a diagram that Brady drew about the factors in the formation of petroleum. Follow the directions.

G. Note-Taking Guide Page

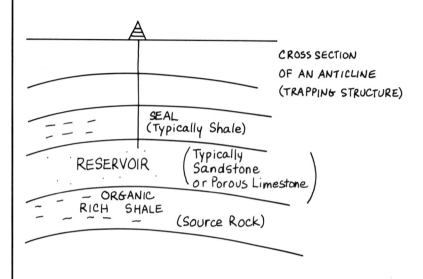

CROSS SECTION
OF AN ANTICLINE
(TRAPPING STRUCTURE)

SEAL
(Typically Shale)

RESERVOIR (Typically Sandstone or Porous Limestone)

— ORGANIC RICH SHALE (Source Rock)

Fig. 9–2 Petroleum Formation

Look at the following list of terms. For source rock, all the information is filled in. On the first line, write the key words for Brady's definition. The second line is for additional information. The diagram will help you understand the mini-lecture. As you listen to the tape, fill in the other items.

1. Source Rock: *rock – organic material/petroleum derived clays, muds, salt water*

2. Reservoir Rock: _____

     _____

3. Migration: _____

     _____

4. Traps:

     Dome: _____ Anticline: _____

5. Stratigraphic Trap: _____

     _____

6. Seal: _____

     _____

H. Review Strategy: Predicting Exam Questions

Look back at page 26 in Lesson 3. Reread the section on predicting exam questions. Write three exam questions to the left of your notes on page 72.

I. Feature of the Lecture: Definitions in Context

The outstanding feature of Brady's lecture is his use of definitions in context. He is able to give the student some idea of the new terms he is using by putting the definition of the new word in the same sentence or in a sentence near it. For example, he says,

There's source rock which is the rock in which the organic material or petroleum is actually derived . . . The trap then is where the petroleum accumulates . . .

Turn to the script for Brady on page 147 and follow the directions given.

J. Comprehension Exercise: True/False

Use your notes to decide whether each of the following statements is *true* or *false*. If the statement is *false*, underline the information that is incorrect. Change this information so that the statement will be true, according to the lecture. Circle *T* for true and *F* for false.

1. *T* *F* Source rock is the rock in which the dome material is derived.

2. *T* *F* The trap is where the petroleum accumulates.

3. *T* *F* A reservoir rock is a porous rock that allows the fluids to flow through it.

4. *T* *F* A dome bends more strongly in one direction.

5. *T* *F* An example from the lecture of a stratigraphic trap is an ancient clay river.

K. Comprehension Exercise: Short Essay

Your teacher will pick one or two of the review questions from Exercise H for you to use as your short essay exercise.

L. Discussion or Written Assignments

1. Think of the different ways that modern society uses oil. Describe some of them.

2. What are the advantages and disadvantages of oil compared to solar or nuclear energy? Make a chart comparing other energy sources with oil and then summarize your chart in paragraph form.

3. How does the price of petroleum products affect the economy of your country? How does it affect the world economy?

4. Find out about a country that relies on oil for its economic survival. Trace oil's effect on the politics of the country.

A. Speaker

Elaine Bennett is an associate professor of economics at the University of Kansas. She received a doctorate in managerial economics and decision science from Northwestern University in 1980. She has been an invited lecturer throughout the United States and in several European countries. She specializes in cooperative and non-cooperative models of multilateral bargaining.

B. Background

Decision making can be a complex process. There often are many variables to consider before a decision can be made. It is also necessary to anticipate the consequences of a decision, including how that decision will affect others. Think about some of the difficult decisions you have made recently.

C. Prelistening Discussion

Bennett will describe some decisions that buyers and sellers have to make. Discuss these questions in small groups or with a classmate.

1. When you buy something, what do you consider?
2. Do you always compare prices before you buy something?
3. What causes the prices of certain goods to change?

D. Prelistening Vocabulary

Before you listen to the lecture, practice the pronunciation of the following key words with your teacher. Notice the syllable in each word with the most important stress.

*General   Read the sentence for each word. For **synonyms**, think of another word or other words that could replace the italicized word. For **other forms**, write in nouns, adjectives, or other word forms of the italicized word.*

1. perspective
   (perSPECtive)

   From the politician's *perspective*, raising taxes was necessary and beneficial. The voters disagreed.

   SYNONYMS: *point of view, position*

   Other forms: *no common ones*

2. optimal
   (OPtimal)

   The *optimal* time for a visit to Washington, D.C., would be in early spring when the weather is mild.

   SYNONYMS: _____

   Other forms: _____

3. maximize
   (MAXimize)

   In order to *maximize* the benefits of travel to another country, it helps to know the language spoken there.

   SYNONYMS: _____

   Other forms: _____

4. focus
   (FOcus)

Because the *focus* of the chapter was international business, there was no information on how companies advertise locally.

SYNONYMS: _____

Other forms: _____

5. grocery store
   (GROcery store)

Grocery stores sell mostly food. However, newer stores also sell flowers, videotapes, medicines, magazines, and even clothes.

SYNONYMS: _____

Other forms: _____

6. interact
   (interACT)

Clerks in stores *interact* with many customers every day while they try to give them efficient, friendly service.

SYNONYMS: _____

Other forms: _____

7. affect
   (afFECT)

Sunshine or rain can *affect* people's moods and make them feel differently.

SYNONYMS: _____

Other forms: _____

Field-specific   *For each of the following words, read the sentence and use the context to guess the definition. Write the meaning in your own words if possible. Note that some of the following words are common in everyday language. It is important to recognize their technical meanings.*

8. microeconomics
   (microecoNOMics)

Macroeconomics deals with the total employment of a country, the total output of goods and services. In contrast, *microeconomics* deals with decisions of individual consumers and other economic units.

MEANING: _____

9. allowance
   (alLOWance)

Some parents give their children an *allowance* each week so that the children begin to learn how to spend money wisely.

MEANING: _____

10. commodities
    (comMODities)

The price of *commodities* such as fresh fruit, clothes, and gasoline can change from one month to the next.

MEANING: _____

11. probabilities
    (probaBILities)

When you calculate the safety of traveling by car or by plane, you need to consider the *probabilities* of accidents.

MEANING: _____

12. estimates
    (EStimates)

Before deciding which mechanic will repair damage to a car, the car owner often gets several *estimates* and compares them.

MEANING: _____

13. approach
    (apPROACH)

His *approach* to solving problems was very practical and thoughtful.

MEANING: _____

14. strategically
    (straTEgically)

New products must be introduced *strategically*; timing and cost are extremely important.

MEANING: _____

15. competing
    (comPETing)

In the championship tournament, four teams were *competing* for the title.

MEANING: _____

16. market
    (MARket)

When advertising a product, firms consider the local, national, and international *markets*.

MEANING: _____

Idioms   *When you listen to a professor explain a concept, some phrases will be new for you. You may stop listening and try to check in your dictionary for a couple of the words. However, if you do this, you may miss the next idea. It's better to continue listening because the meaning may become clearer later. In Bennett's explanation, she uses several expressions with the verb* **take***. Look at the following contexts and guess the meaning of the expressions.*

17. taking all the rest
    of the world
    as given

In math, we know the circumference of a circle equals 360 degrees. We know that is a given quantity. We also *take* some prices *as given*. We believe that tax laws will not change every year, and so we invest money to take advantage of those laws.

MEANING: _____

18. take into account

Susan and her husband Bill were planning a short vacation. There were many factors to consider. They had to decide where to go, how to get there, how long to stay in each place, and how much money to spend. They also needed to *take into account* the fact that hotels and planes would fill up very fast at vacation time.

MEANING: _____

What do you *take into account* in each of these situations?

a. renting an apartment _____

b. choosing a major _____

c. buying a car _____

d. riding a bicycle _____

e. getting a divorce _____

f. using a computer _____

19. take those into account

"If you don't know whether your boss is going to fire you or not, you make probability estimates on those things and *take those* into account."

MEANING: _____

What does Bennett mean by "those"? _____

_____

20. act accordingly

As John was driving to work, he saw an accident in front of him. A car had hit a motorcycle. John stopped to see if he could help. The rider of the motorcycle was on the ground, and he looked hurt. He couldn't move his leg. The driver of the car was not injured, but he seemed very upset. John saw that they needed an ambulance and so he *acted accordingly*. He got back in his car and went to call the police so they could send for an ambulance.

MEANING: _____

E. Note-Taking Techniques: 1. Extended Examples
2. Personal Examples

1. Extended Examples

In this lecture, Bennett will describe decision making from two different perspectives: game theory and microeconomics. She will offer several examples for each perspective. Her examples will help you imagine the situation.

Refer back to your notes in Lessons 1 and 4 to review headings.

2. Personal Examples

In addition to noting the examples Bennett gives in her lecture, you should try to add one more step. Earlier in the text you practiced writing your own examples to help you remember concepts in the lecture. Here is another opportunity to do this.

Listen to your teacher give a short explanation. While you listen, write down notes on the lines given. On the left side of the page, write a word or phrase to remind you of a personal experience or example. You did this type of exercise in Lessons 7 and 8, on the adjustment of students.

Consumer Choices

_____

_____

_____

_____

_____

_____

⊙⊙ F. Main Idea/Organization Check

Read through these questions or statements before you listen to the tape. As you listen to the lecture for the first time, listen for the main ideas. Circle the letter of the best answer.

This is not a note-taking exercise. You will have a chance to take notes on the material later.

1. Which perspective does Bennett explain first?
   a. microeconomics
   b. game theory
   c. macroeconomics

2. She uses the example of spending money on pizza to show _____.
   a. a strategic interaction
   b. an individual's decision
   c. an unnecessary decision

3. How does Bennett signal that she is going to begin to talk about the second perspective?
   a. "and this is where game theory changes"
   b. "and this is where microeconomics differs"
   c. "and this is where game theory is different"

4. What is the key concept of a game theory approach to decision making?
   a. interaction
   b. individualism
   c. intervention

G. Note-Taking Guide Page

Date: _____

Microeconomics

Game Theory

Summary:

H. Note-Taking Technique

3. Writing the Summary Statement

Bennett's extended examples seem like the introduction to a longer lecture. At the end of an introduction or at the end of a lecture, professors will often wrap up or summarize in a sentence or two the main points they have explained. This type of summary should be written down so that you can see it easily as you review for quizzes and tests.

Bennett begins her summary with the word *thus*. When you heard this word at the end of the lecture, what did you write as the summary? Did you get most of the words? What did you abbreviate?

I. Review Strategy: Analyzing Situations and Applying Principles

One good way to study concepts is to see if you can apply them to other situations and understand how they work. Consider these situations. Explain which people or groups would need to interact and what they should consider before making a decision.

1. buying a new coat _____

2. quitting a job _____

3. advertising a new product _____

4. getting married _____

5. investing money _____

6. buying oil _____

7. choosing a major field of study _____

J. Features of the Lecture: 1. Rephrasing Ideas
2. Use of Conditionals

1. Rephrasing Ideas

When professors think and add examples as they explain, they sometimes begin a sentence and change it because a better idea comes to mind. This rephrasing often results in sentences that would be ungrammatical in written form. Native speakers can understand the meaning of these sentences easily. It is more difficult for non-native speakers.

2. Use of Conditionals

When we discuss strategy, we are always considering the possible actions of another person or group involved in a situation. Consider this situation.

A construction company wants to cut down the trees in a local forest so that new office buildings can be built there.

Complete each of these conditional statements. Use your imagination to create different answers.

If they cut down the trees, _____

If new offices go in, executives _____

If the citizens of the area complain, _____

_____

The forest could be preserved if _____

If this happened near my city, people _____

Turn to the script for Bennett on page 149 and follow the directions given.

K. Discussion or Written Assignments

1. From a local newspaper, find a short article that describes decisions people had to make (i.e., a court case, election, family matter, or business merger). What did each person or group need to consider before making the decision?

2. Look at some advertisements for popular commodities such as cars, clothes, appliances, or food. Try to think of the ad from the advertising manager's point of view. Why should this ad increase sales? Have you seen any other similar ads for competitive products? What type of ads are the most effective?

3. With your classmates, you will act out a trading day at a flea market. A flea market is a place where people buy and sell new and used goods. Prices are not fixed as they are in stores. Bargaining is possible. Your teacher will give you a role. Some of you will try to buy a radio, and others will have radios to sell. You will each have a price in mind. As trading continues, your teacher or another student will keep track of the purchases that are made and at what prices. After the trading is over, discuss how the buyers and sellers interacted.

Discussion Notes

_____

_____

_____

_____

_____

_____

_____

_____

_____

LESSON
11 / Automatic Feedback Control Systems

A. Speaker

James R. Rowland is professor and department chairman of electrical and computer engineering at the University of Kansas. He has a doctorate in electrical engineering from Purdue University and has held faculty appointments at Georgia Institute of Technology in Atlanta and at Oklahoma State University. The author of a textbook on linear control systems, Rowland has been active in engineering education circles for many years.

B. Background

A major focus of electrical engineering is the design and service of electronic devices, which include timers, stereo components, and appliances. These devices are made up of complex circuits and systems. An electrical engineer must analyze the situation that requires an electronic device to decide which particular system will give the desired results.

C. Prelistening Discussion

In many of our homes, the number of automatic appliances is increasing. Nowadays, it is common to see a private home that has several appliances in it. These can include microwave ovens, washers and dryers, air conditioners, toasters, and phone-answering machines.

1. Which automatic appliances seem the most popular today?
2. Are these appliances necessary?
3. Do you know how any automatic appliances work?

D. Prelistening Vocabulary

Before you listen to the lecture, practice the pronunciation of the following key words with your teacher. Notice the syllable in each word with the most important stress.

General   *Read the sentence for each word. For* **synonyms**, *think of another word or other words that could replace the italicized word. For* **other forms**, *write in nouns, adjectives, or other word forms of the italicized word.*

1. applications
   (appliCAtions)

In recent years, people have discovered new *applications* for laser technology, such as eye surgery and inventory control.

SYNONYMS: _____ *uses* _____

Other forms: _____ *apply, applied, applicator* _____

2. variable
   (VARiable)

The success of the project depends on a number of *variables*, such as the manager's skill and the cost of materials.

SYNONYMS: _____

Other forms: _____

85

3. disturbance
(disTURBance)

The loud music down the hall was a *disturbance* to the neighbors who were studying for exams.

SYNONYMS: _____

Other forms: _____

4. moisture
(MOISture)

When there is a lot of *moisture* in the air, we say it's very humid or sticky.

SYNONYMS: _____

Other forms: _____

5. expense
(exPENSE)

The cost of room and board is an *expense* that varies from university to university.

SYNONYMS: _____

Other forms: _____

Field-specific *For each of the following words, read the sentence and use the context to guess the definition. Write the meaning in your own words if possible.*

6. feedback
(FEEDback)

When the sound engineer adjusts the microphones for a concert, a loud, high-pitched *feedback* sometimes can be heard.

MEANING: _____

7. input
(INput)

Check your *input*; maybe you entered the data incorrectly.

MEANING: _____

8. output
(OUTput)

The *output* of a machine may refer to such things as electricity, heat, light, or cool air.

MEANING: _____

9. loop
(LOOP)

You need to write a *loop* into your program so that you can repeat a series of commands.

MEANING: _____

10. sensor
(SENsor)

The camera has a *sensor* that responds to light and will give you a signal if the room is too dark for filming.

MEANING: _____

11. rudder
(RUDder)

If the *rudder* is not functioning properly, a ship might go off course.

MEANING: _____

12. lawn sprinkler
    (LAWN SPRINkler)

In summer, you can see *lawn sprinklers* on when you walk across campus. Sometimes you have to walk around a certain area if you don't want to get wet.

MEANING: _____

E. Note-Taking Technique: Using Parallel Headings

Rowland's lecture explains two types of systems. For this type of information, you will probably want to use some parallel headings. Review the suggestions in Lesson 3 on separate or side-by-side headings. It will be necessary to understand how the systems function differently. Review your notes on page 25 to see which style you used the last time. Use the style that will allow you to write faster.

F. Main Idea/Organization Check

Read through these questions or statements before you listen to the tape. As you listen to the lecture for the first time, listen for the main ideas. Circle the letter of the best answer.

This is not a note-taking exercise. You will have a chance to take notes later.

1. What information does Rowland give in his introduction?
   a. the definition of feedback
   b. the advantages of a closed-loop system
   c. the description of an aircraft

2. What does the next section of his lecture list?
   a. the disadvantages of feedback systems
   b. the components of the two systems
   c. the price of the open-loop controller

3. In his discussion of an open-loop system, Rowland mentions pre-set conditions. How do these conditions relate to open-loop systems?
   a. are not related
   b. require extra expense
   c. control the output

4. Which type of system does Rowland feel is more costly and more complicated?
   a. open-loop
   b. closed-loop
   c. lighting

5. Rowland concludes his lecture by _____.
   a. asking students to volunteer
   b. giving a formal summary
   c. previewing the next topic

6. Which subtopics will be important to list in your outline?
   a. open- and closed-loop systems
   b. components, cost, use
   c. clothes dryers and toasters

NOTE: You will not have any formal outline to follow for this lecture. On the note-taking page, there is a diagram similar to one you might find in a text or on the board in class. Some of the parts are already labeled. Label the others as you listen.

Remember to use some of the techniques from earlier lessons: abbreviations, parallel headings, indenting, blank space, lists, and diagrams.

Use the blank page to add your notes.

G. Note-Taking Guide Page

Date: _____

_____

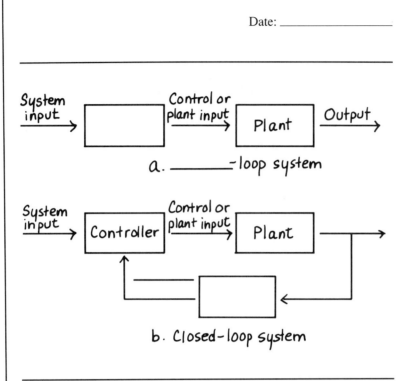

a. _____-loop system

b. Closed-loop system

Fig. 11–1 Open- and Closed-loop Systems

☐ From James R. Rowland, *Linear Control Systems: Modeling, Analysis, and Design*, 8. New York: John Wiley & Sons, 1986.

H. Review Strategies: 1. Highlighting Key Points
2. Making Charts

1. Highlighting Key Points

After class, try to review your notes when you can. As you review, you can add more information that you still remember from class. You can make the main points stand out by using a colored pen or pencil to underline or draw a box around the main points. We call this process of making marks *highlighting*. There are also special pens that allow you to draw a line over words and still read them. Some students hesitate to use this technique in textbooks. In your own notes, however, you should feel free to make any marks that will help you review.

2. Making Charts

You have already reviewed material by writing practice exam questions in the margin. Another technique that helps us to summarize information is making a chart with the main points. You can put these charts right in your notebook.

a. Use your notes from Rowland's lecture to fill in the boxes in the following chart. When you write notes in the boxes, you will have a quick summary of the information in Rowland's lecture.

Review Chart

	plant	controller	cost	performance	ex.
OPEN LOOP					
CLOSED LOOP					

b. Think of the examples Rowland gave in his lecture. Design a small chart to help you remember which appliances have open-loop control systems and which ones have closed-loop systems. Give the reasons, too.

c. Rowland also listed several examples of input and output. Organize these examples into a small chart. Using charts like this can help you review for quizzes.

If you do this type of review on your own, you will find out which sections of the textbook you need to review. What is another advantage of using a system like this to summarize information? Are there any disadvantages?

⊙⊙   I. Features of the Lecture: 1. Repetition of Key Words
2. Intonation of Parallel Ideas
3. Rhetorical Questions

1. Repetition of Key Words

In several of the previous lessons, you have noted the key words and the stress on them. Rowland repeats some of his key words, especially in his introduction. This is very common when professors want to make sure that students are following them at the beginning of the lecture.

2. Intonation of Parallel Ideas

You have listened for contrastive stress in some of the other lectures. In Rowland's lecture, you can hear the intonation pattern that is used to explain parallel ideas. The nouns, adjectives, or phrases will get the same type of stress when the ideas are very parallel.

Read these sentences aloud. Underline the parallel structures.

1. The professor collected our assignments and then handed out our test papers.
2. When it's time for vacation, students go to the beach, families go camping, and some people just go to sleep.
3. California is famous for its beaches, its movie stars, and its universities.

Now answer these questions. Use parallel structures.

4. Why do people prefer to live in cities?

_____

_____

5. What did you do last Saturday?

_____

_____

3. Rhetorical Questions

During a lecture, a professor may ask one student a question. In large classes, however, that is often not practical. A professor sometimes asks rhetorical questions, those questions that do not require a direct answer. These questions help all the students to think about a topic or an issue in the discussion. The professor may often answer the question without waiting for an answer from a student.

Turn to the script for Rowland on page 151 and follow the directions given.

J. Comprehension Exercise: True/False

Use your notes to decide whether each of the following statements is *true* or *false*. If the statement is *false*, underline the information that is incorrect. Change this information so that the statement will be true, according to the lecture. Circle *T* for true and *F* for false.

1. *T*   *F*   Feedback is the use of a system's output to change the input for purposes of control.

2. *T*   *F*   A controller is used in both open- and closed-loop systems.

3. *T*   *F*   An open-loop system is more complex than a closed-loop one.

4. *T*   *F*   One advantage of the open-loop system is its low cost.

5. *T*   *F*   Toasters are controlled by sensors.

6. *T*   *F*   Closed-loop systems are more sensitive to disturbance.

91

7. *T*   *F*   An elevator has an open-loop system for feedback control.

8. *T*   *F*   A clothes dryer has a sensor for moisture.

9. *T*   *F*   The term *automatic* always involves a type of sensor.

10. *T*   *F*   Rowland suggests an open-loop system in situations with little chance for great amounts of disturbance.

K. Comprehension Exercise: Short Essay

Choose one or two of the following topics. For each one, write a paragraph using information from your notes.

1. Define feedback as it relates to a control system.
2. List the advantages of an open-loop system.
3. What are some of the disadvantages of a closed-loop system?
4. Explain why a toaster is an example of an open-loop control system.
5. Explain why a home heating system is an example of a closed-loop control system.

L. Discussion or Written Assignments

1. Besides household appliances, what other devices use automatic control systems? What happens when these systems fail?

2. In an encyclopedia or engineering textbook, find a diagram of an appliance or device. Look for the control system. Explain to a classmate which type of control system the device uses.

3. How are people's lives changing because of automatic appliances and devices? What should appliances of the future do for us? Imagine your dream kitchen or living room. Think about the year 2050; what tasks will machines do for us then?

Discussion Notes

12/ A Revolution in Gardening

A. Speaker

Judith K. Major is an assistant professor in the School of Architecture and Urban Design at the University of Kansas. She received a master's degree in landscape architecture in 1977 and is a Ph.D. candidate in architecture at the University of Pennsylvania, with a field of specialization in eighteenth- and nineteenth-century English and American landscape gardening theories.

B. Background

In cities, near some buildings, we can find parks and gardens. As we walk through these gardens, we get an idea of the importance of space and design in that particular society. It is a landscape architect's job to work with the many elements of nature, such as trees, water, rocks, flowers, grass, and open space, in order to create a pleasant place.

C. Prelistening Discussion

In this lecture, you will hear a description of two different styles of gardening. Think for a minute about the purpose of gardens.

1. Are gardens necessary? Why or why not?
2. How can a garden be useful?
3. What makes a wonderful garden?
4. Have you seen any beautiful private or public gardens? Where did you see them? Describe them.

D. Prelistening Vocabulary

Before you listen to the lecture, practice the pronunciation of the following key words with your teacher. Notice the syllable in each word with the most important stress.

*General   Read the sentence for each word. For **synonyms**, think of another word or other words that could replace the italicized word. For **other forms**, write in nouns, adjectives, or other word forms of the italicized word.*

1. era
   (ERa)

   People will remember the 1980s and 1990s as the computer *era* because so much new technology became popular at that time.

   SYNONYMS: *age, period, years*

   Other forms: *none*

2. react against
   (reACT aGAINST)

   When a person gives a strong political opinion, other people may *react against* it.

   SYNONYMS: _____

   Other forms: _____

3. symmetrical
   (symMETrical)

When you look at the wings of a butterfly, the colors and shapes are identical on each side. The pattern is *symmetrical*.

SYNONYMS: _____

Other forms: _____

4. artificial
   (artiFIcial)

In many processed foods, we can find *artificial* sweeteners and colors. Cheese, for example, is yellow or white, but with added color, it looks orange.

SYNONYMS: _____

Other forms: _____

5. clipped
   (CLIPPED)

As she read the newspaper, the teacher *clipped* out articles to save and use with her students. She didn't want to save the whole newspaper.

SYNONYMS: _____

Other forms: _____

6. regard
   (reGARD)

The spectators at the game left trash and papers all over the field, with no *regard* for the beauty of the park.

SYNONYMS: _____

Other forms: _____

7. curved
   (CURVED)

A spoon has *curved* edges; a fork does not.

SYNONYMS: _____

Other forms: _____

8. spontaneity
   (spontaNEity)

The vacationers didn't plan every minute of their trip. *Spontaneity* was important to them.

SYNONYMS: _____

Other forms: _____

9. hostility
   (hosTILity)

Before two countries go to war, a lot of *hostility* usually develops because of political or economic problems.

SYNONYMS: _____

Other forms: _____

10. aristocracy
    (arisTOCracy)

Historically, the *aristocracy* consisted of the royal family and other wealthy or prominent families who owned much of the land or industry in a country.

SYNONYMS: _____

Other forms: _____

11. appropriate
    (apPROpriate)

In the United States, it is *appropriate* to phone someone if you are going to be fifteen minutes late for an appointment.

SYNONYMS: _____

Other forms: _____

12. display
    (disPLAY)

Department stores *display* new products in windows near the sidewalk so that people will want to come in and look around.

SYNONYMS: _____

Other forms: _____

Field-specific *For each of the following words, read the sentence and use the context to guess the definition. Write the meaning in your own words if possible.*

13. landscape gardening
    (LANDscape GARdening)

Landscape gardening seems like a good field for Steve because he loves working with trees and plants and has training in design.

MEANING: _____

14. lawns
    (LAWNS)

Professional gardeners usually care for the *lawns* in public parks and near museums. They water and cut the grass regularly.

MEANING: _____

15. greensward
    (GREENsward)

Greensward is an English name for a large lawn similar to a golf course.

MEANING: _____

16. reforesting
    (reFOResting)

After a fire destroys part of a national park, the government may give money for *reforesting* efforts.

MEANING: _____

17. arable land
    (ARable LAND)

Farming areas are those places in a country with *arable land* for growing grain, vegetables, and other crops.

MEANING: _____

18. aesthetic
    (aesTHETic)

The statue had little *aesthetic* value; no one thought it was beautiful and many people said it had no meaning.

MEANING: _____

Defined By the Lecturer In Brady's lecture, you heard some definitions in the same sentence as the new term. Major also defines several terms for the students. She uses the expressions *what came to be known as* and which was called *to indicate these definitions.*

To define the art of topiary, Major first gives some characteristics of this style. She begins with the definition instead of the term itself. This is a challenge for a notetaker. You have to quickly jot down or write the definition. At the time you hear the characteristics, you may not realize that they will be important. After the definition, Major goes on to give an additional example. This gives you time to add notes to your definition.

Listen as your teacher reads this short section from Major's lecture. Fill in the missing words. Some are part of the phrases mentioned above.

. . . the vegetation was carved into very artificial shapes, and _____ was _____ the art of topiary, _____ vegetation was clipped and pruned sometimes into fantastic animal _____ .

Which word that you added signals the example? _____

E. Note-Taking Technique: 1. Writing Preview Questions

Look at the title of the lecture. Think of three questions that you think Major might answer.

Ex. When did this revolution happen?   Who did the gardening?

Write your three questions at the top of page 100. As the lecturer speaks, listen for the answers to your questions.

⊙⊙ ## F. Main Idea/Organization Check

Read through these questions or statements before you listen to the tape. As you listen to the lecture for the first time, listen for the main ideas. Circle the letter of the best answer.

This is not a note-taking exercise. You will have a chance to take notes later.

1. What kind of information does Major give?
   a. architectural
   b. historical
   c. emotional

2. What does the first part of her lecture describe?
   a. the design of French gardens
   b. American gardening tastes
   c. the style of English gardens

3. How did she describe English gardens?
   a. geometrical
   b. natural
   c. artificial

4. According to Major, why were trees important in England in the eighteenth century?
   a. for shipbuilding
   b. for architecture
   c. for farming

5. Major uses many different words to describe the timber shortage in England. Which phrase below does not apply to that situation?
   a. devastation of the land
   b. demolishing trees
   c. the country house emerged

G. Note-Taking Technique: 2. Recognizing Development of the Topic

Even in a very short lecture, several aspects of a topic can be discussed. In order to take notes that are organized and useful for review, it is necessary to recognize main points as the lecturer gives them.

As you take your own notes on Major's lecture, be sure to label the information carefully. How does she divide the information that she gives? What are the three aspects of the topic that she explains?

Aspect of the Topic	*Phrase Used to Signal a New Kind of Information*
1. _____	*some of the characteristics . . .*
2. _____	*at the beginning of the century . . .* *in contrast to this . . .*
3. _____	*for a number of reasons . . .*

Listen for these signals to help you see the development of her ideas. When you hear these signals, you should write a new heading in your notes, indent, or leave room for a list.

H. Note-Taking Guide Page

Date: _____

A REVOLUTION IN GARDENING

Preview Questions

Ex. When did this revolution occur?

1. _____

2. _____

3. _____

_____

FRENCH AND DUTCH GARDENS

a. _____

b. symmetrical

c. _____

d. _____

ENGLISH

a. sweeping lawns

b. _____

REASONS FOR THE CHANGE

a. cultivated landscape was ideal

  natural = wild

b. _____

c. John Evelyn

d. _____

e. _____

f. political reasons

  William Kent

I. Review Strategies: 1. Drawing Pictures
2. Answering Preview Questions

1. Drawing Pictures

Go back to your notes. Read the characteristics of the French garden and the English garden. In the space on the left side on page 100, draw a simple garden that shows the characteristics Major described. These little pictures will help you remember the differences between the two styles.

2. Answering Preview Questions

Look at your preview questions on page 100. Also look at the two sample questions in Exercise E. Jot down a few words to answer each question. Now rearrange your answers into one informative paragraph. On another piece of paper, write this summary to help you review later.

J. Features of the Lecture: 1. Listing Intonation
2. Use of Pronouns
3. Elaboration of a Point

1. Listing Intonation

Major gave many characteristics of both French and English gardens in her lecture. From her voice, you can tell that she is going to mention several ideas. Her voice does not drop at the end of each characteristic. Instead, the pauses are very short and her voice goes up a bit to signal that she will mention something else that belongs in the list of characteristics.

2. Use of Pronouns

To refer back to a whole idea or situation previously described, a professor will often use indefinite pronouns such as *this* or *it*. In order to take notes on these generalizations, it is important to understand the original reference for these pronouns. You already use this skill in reading. It is more difficult to understand pronoun reference when you are listening because, unless you record a speech, you can't go back over the material again.

Read this paragraph carefully.

> Unemployment has risen in the last few years. Many people do not have the skills they need to find jobs that will pay well. It is difficult for the unemployed to get training because such courses are often expensive. Unless *this* changes, the unemployment situation will worsen.

To what does *this* refer? _____

3. Elaboration of a Point

In Major's lecture, she speaks at length about the situation of forests. She gives this as one cause of the revolution in gardening tastes. To develop this point about the timber shortage, Major refers to trees and the land in many different ways. As you listen to a lecture, it's important to recognize that a professor will give details about, or elaborate on, each point.

Turn to the script for Major on page 153 and follow the directions given.

K. Comprehension Exercise: True/False

Use your notes to decide whether each of the following statements is *true* or *false*. If the statement is *false*, underline the information that is incorrect. Change this information so that the statement will be true, according to the lecture. Circle *T* for true and *F* for false.

1. *T*   *F*   French gardens of the eighteenth century were very formal.

2. *T*   *F*   Carving trees into strange shapes was called cultivation.

3. *T*   *F*   The lawns of English gardens were very symmetrical in design.

4. *T*   *F*   Forests in England increased because the navy needed wood for ships.

5. *T*   *F*   Country homes became popular because people had more money to spend.

6. *T*   *F*   John Evelyn influenced the English people by designing a natural type of garden.

7. *T*   *F*   The growth of cities brought problems and made people feel the need to escape.

8. *T*   *F*   In the English style of landscape gardening, trees represented the hostility and wildness of nature.

9. *T*   *F*   The English people rejected the French style of gardens partly because England was moving toward a more democratic form of government.

10. *T*   *F*   William Kent was a landscape designer who respected the beauty of natural gardens.

L. Comprehension Exercise: Short Essay

Choose one or two of the following topics. For each one, write a paragraph using information from your notes.

1. What is the main difference between a seventeenth-century French garden and an eighteenth-century English one?
2. Give two causes for the revolution in landscape gardening in the eighteenth century.
3. Do you prefer natural landscapes or cultivated ones? Explain your preference.

M. Discussion or Written Assignments

1. How is landscape gardening important in cities? in the country?

2. Do gardens in your city or country resemble the ones Major described? How are they different?

3. Have there been some changes in the architecture or in the landscape gardening in your city in recent years? How is the landscape different now? Are these changes good? Who or what caused the changes?

4. Collect or take pictures of some gardens or other landscapes and compare them. How is nature important in each picture? How do you feel when you see each place? What would you do if you went to that place?

5. Take a walk in a garden in your city. Write a paragraph to describe this garden to someone else. How did you feel? Did you like the garden? Why or why not?

6. There are also revolutions in styles of clothing and architecture. Discuss the reasons for these changes in different eras and in different places. Make a chart with the time and the changes and the reasons. Do this in a small group.

7. Major talked about the deforesting in England. There were not enough trees. Wood is an important resource in many countries. What other resources should we try to protect? What do we use these resources for? What will happen if these resources run out?

Discussion Notes

_____

_____

_____

_____

_____

_____

_____

_____

_____

_____

_____

_____

_____

_____

_____

_____

_____

LESSON
13/ Why Leaves Change Color

A. Speaker

Craig Martin is an associate professor of botany at the University of Kansas. He has a doctorate in botany from Duke University. Since arriving at the University of Kansas in 1980, he has established an active research program in the area of ecological plant physiology, specializing in studies of plant photosynthesis. His studies of weeds, grasses, prairie plants, succulents, and tropical epiphytes have taken him throughout Kansas, to the Everglades of Florida, to Germany, and to the heart of Africa.

B. Background

In many parts of the world, there are only two seasons. In the United States, however, many parts of the country experience four seasons. As the climate changes, trees and flowers go through different stages of growth.

C. Prelistening Discussion

In this lecture, you will hear about the leaves of autumn and why they change color. Think about the environment in which you live and the changes you see during different times of the year.

1. How many seasons are there in your city?
2. What is the weather like during the different seasons?
3. Which season do you prefer and why?
4. Do the leaves on the trees in your neighborhood change color?

D. Prelistening Vocabulary

Before you listen to the lecture, practice the pronunciation of the following key words with your teacher. Notice the syllable in each word with the most important stress.

General   *Read the sentence for each word. For **synonyms**, think of another word or other words that could replace the italicized word. For **other forms**, write in nouns, adjectives, or other word forms of the italicized word.*

1. mechanisms
   (MECHanisms)

   A public election is one of the *mechanisms* used to choose a new president.

   SYNONYMS: _ways, processes_

   Other forms: _mechanical, mechanic_

2. underlie
   (underLIE)

   One condition that *underlies* the change in women's role in society is better education.

   SYNONYMS: _____

   Other forms: _____

105

3. synthesize
   (SYNthesize)

For an exam, you must be able to *synthesize* information from your notes, class lectures, and the text.

SYNONYMS: _____

Other forms: _____

4. conversion
   (conVERsion)

What is the *conversion* rate for dollars and francs?

SYNONYMS: _____

Other forms: _____

5. relatively
   (RELatively)

The temperature last month was *relatively* high; 55 degrees instead of the usual 38.

SYNONYMS: _____

Other forms: _____

6. regardless
   (reGARDless)

He needs to buy that state-of-the-art equipment *regardless* of the cost.

SYNONYMS: _____

Other forms: _____

7. drought
   (DROUGHT)

When there is a *drought*, farmers have to spend more time and money on irrigation.

SYNONYMS: _____

Other forms: _____

8. maple
   (MAple)

A red *maple* leaf is used on the national flag of Canada.

SYNONYMS: _____

Other forms: _____

Field-specific   *For each of the following words, read the sentence and use the context to guess the definition. Write the meaning in your own words.*

9. hormones
   (HORmones)

Insulin is one of many *hormones* that are produced within our bodies to keep our organs functioning properly.

MEANING: _____

10. pigment
    (PIGment)

Without *pigment*, leaves, flowers, animals, and people would be colorless.

MEANING: _____

11. chlorophyll
    (CHLOrophyll)

Chlorophyll gives green color to leaves and plants.

MEANING: _____

12. sugars
    (SUgars)

Glucose and fructose are types of *sugars*.

MEANING: _____

13. photosynthesis
    (photoSYNthesis)

Because of *photosynthesis*, plants can use light and water to grow and develop.

MEANING: _____

14. environmental factors
    (environMENTal FACtors)

In the growth of plants, *environmental factors* to be considered include water, light, humidity, and insects.

MEANING: _____

E. Note-Taking Technique: 1. Writing Preview Questions

Look at the topic of the lecture. At the top of page 110, write three questions that you think Martin will answer in his lecture.

Ex. Do all leaves change color at the same time of year?
How is rain important in the changing of leaves?

⊙⊙ F. Main Idea/Organization Check

Read through these questions or statements before you listen to the tape. As you listen to the lecture for the first time, listen for the main ideas. Circle the letter of the best answer.

This is not a note-taking exercise. You will have a chance to take notes on the material later.

1. How does Martin introduce his topic?
   a. "I would like to talk about . . ."
   b. "Let's take a look at . . ."
   c. "There are many factors that . . ."

2. What is the main focus in the first part of the lecture?
   a. names of many Kansas trees
   b. changes in the pigment in leaves
   c. why temperatures change in the fall

3. What is the "synthesis" that Martin mentions?
   a. making of the red pigment from sugars
   b. understanding all environmental factors
   c. disappearance of the green pigment

107

4. In the situation Martin describes, which conditions can cause damage to the leaves?
   a. drought and warm days
   b. cool nights and drought
   c. frost and severe drought

5. Which tree turns bright red every year, no matter what the environmental conditions are?
   a. maple
   b. sumac
   c. elm

G. Note-Taking Techniques: 2. Recognizing and Listing Causes
3. Writing Unfamiliar Words

2. Recognizing and Listing Causes

Throughout Martin's lecture, he is explaining the causes of certain changes in the color of leaves. At the beginning of his lecture, he explains how leaves turn yellow. What does he describe in the last two-thirds of his lecture?

It is difficult to take notes on causes and effects even though it is one of the most common patterns of organization. The pattern is complex because you have to understand a lot of information very quickly. If you are in a large lecture hall, it is not always possible to stop a professor to ask for clarification.

Like many other professors, Martin uses a variety of phrases to indicate cause and effect. As you listen, it is important to recognize some key phrases that signal explanation of a cause. These phrases include:

- influence the change
- respond to these changes by
- cause various . . . to
- is a result of
- for that very reason
- is stimulated by
- if . . . then there should be

In order to successfully note details of causes and effects, you have to write quickly. You will need to use some kind of symbol or abbreviation to show which information is the cause and which is the effect.

One common way to do this is to use an arrow (———>). The arrow will always begin next to the cause and point in the direction of the effect.

Ex. 1. Freezing temperatures will result in severe damage to the citrus trees.

   frzing temps ———> damage citr. trees

Sometimes the professor will mention the effect first, and then you can draw the arrow in the opposite direction. You will need to write down the key words quickly and add the arrows later.

Ex. 2. Hotter summer temperatures have been caused by the damage to the ozone layer.

   hot sum. temps <——— damage ozne

What is another way to indicate cause and effect in your notes?

3. Writing Unfamiliar Words

When professors lecture, they often write new terms on the chalkboard so that students can write them in their notes. Some professors, however, use the board very little. If you are listening to a lecture and you hear many new terms or concepts, what are some of the ways you can get the correct spelling in your notes?

Here are a couple of ways to avoid hesitating when you hear a difficult word or phrase.

a. Try to write the first three or four letters. Then draw a line for the rest of the word. This blank line will help you remember to go back and fill it in later. The same term may be mentioned again and you can go back during the lecture and write a few more letters of the word.

   Ex. metam_____ (for metamorphosis)

b. You can also start to write a word and then put a question mark (?) next to it in the notes. After class, ask the professor or a classmate or check in your textbook.

   Ex. metam (?) (for metamorphosis)

Practice writing the first letters of some difficult words. Your teacher or your classmates will use each word in a sentence. Use one of the techniques discussed to help you write as much of the word as possible.

1. _____

2. _____

3. _____

4. _____

5. _____

As you listen to Martin's lecture, try to write down parts of the botanical terms and the names of trees that are unfamiliar to you. Notice how he repeats some of the words many times. When you hear a difficult word again later in the lecture, try to complete its spelling in your notes.

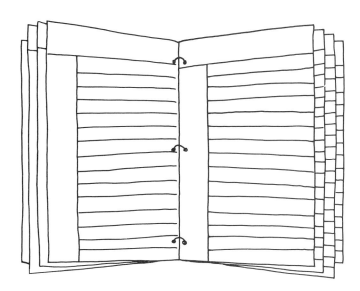

Lesson 13

H. Note-Taking Guide Page

Why Leaves Change Color

Preview Questions

Ex. *How is rain important in the changing of leaves?*

1. _____

2. _____

3. _____

_____

THE MECHANISMS

    green pigment

    yellow pigment

    red pigment

II. Environmental Conditions   ⟶   synthesis

1. _____

2. _____

3. _____

III. 1986 Conditions

I. Review Strategies: 1. Answering Preview Questions
2. Summarizing a Process

1. Answering Preview Questions

Go back to the questions you wrote before you listened to the lecture. Did Martin answer your questions? Find the information in your notes and jot down a word or two near your question. If he did not answer your questions, where could you find the answers?

2. Summarizing a Process

a. Look back at your notes and locate the section on how the leaves turn yellow. Expand your notes into a couple of sentences to explain this process. Write these sentences on the left third of your note-taking page or at the end of your notes.
b. Find the section in your notes on the development of the red pigment in leaves. Write a few complete sentences to explain the mechanism for the production of the red pigment. Be sure to mention which environmental conditions help this process. Write this information at the end of your notes. Label this summary *HOW RED PIGMENT DEVELOPS*.

J. Features of the Lecture: 1. Rephrasing
2. Fast Speech

1. Rephrasing

Professors rephrase their ideas for several reasons. They may decide to clarify the previous idea mentioned. In other cases, if they know the concept is difficult for students to understand, they will try to rephrase the idea in a simpler way. Once in a while, a professor may misspeak and actually say the information incorrectly. Rephrasings happen at this point to correct previous information given to students. While professors are thinking, they may rephrase their last idea so that it connects better to the next point. If a student asks a question in class, the professor will often rephrase some information already given.

Martin rephrases information to make it clearer. Usually, these rephrasings are synonyms that directly follow the adjective or noun.

". . . the green pigment, chlorophyll, . . ."

Another signal in Martin's lecture is the use of phrases such as *in other words* and the use of *when* to indicate an example of something he has just said.

". . . if it's been a good year for the tree, um . . . in other words, they've photosynthesized a lot, . . ."

2. Fast Speech

Throughout Martin's lecture, he gives a lot of information very quickly. Because this is his area of specialization, he has probably explained this process many times before.

When your professor speaks quickly, try not to become discouraged. There may be some ideas that you don't catch the first time, and you'll need to listen for the rephrasing. If this is still difficult for you, there are some other ways you can cope with the fast speech.

1. Sit near the front of the class so that you can hear better.
2. Find a study partner in the class. Compare notes with this student to clarify the questions in your notes.

Lesson 13

3. Take a small tape recorder to class and record the lecture. Be sure to get the professor's permission first. Use this to go back over your notes and add more information.

What else can you do if the professor speaks very fast?

4. _____

5. _____

6. _____

Turn to the script for Martin on page 155 and follow the directions given.

K. Comprehension Exercise: True/False

Use your notes to decide whether each of the following statements is *true* or *false*. If the statement is *false*, underline the information that is incorrect. Change this information so that the statement will be true, according to the lecture. Circle *T* for true and *F* for false.

1. *T* *F* Another name for the green pigment in leaves is chlorophyll.

2. *T* *F* When the chlorophyll appears, the leaves on elm and hickory trees look yellow.

3. *T* *F* Synthesis of a red pigment is stimulated by changes in environmental conditions.

4. *T* *F* The sugar in the leaves becomes a green pigment.

5. *T* *F* For leaves to turn bright red, the daytime temperature must be very cool and the nighttime temperature must be warm.

6. *T* *F* Freezing temperatures will cause damage to leaves about to change color.

7. *T* *F* Sunny days help leaves change to brighter colors.

8. *T* *F* The sumac and maple always turn red in autumn.

9. *T* *F* When conditions are too wet or cold, the leaves will not turn bright red.

L. Comprehension Exercise: Short Essay

Choose one or two of the following topics. For each one, write a paragraph using information from your notes.

1. Martin mentioned three different kinds of pigment. Give the name and color of each one. Then give an example of a plant or tree in which we can see this pigment.
2. How does sugar develop in the leaves?
3. What is the relationship between photosynthesis and the appearance of red leaves?
4. List the environmental conditions that affect the color of leaves in the autumn.

M. Discussion or Written Assignments

1. Take a walk and look at some trees near your classroom building. Notice the color of the leaves and try to determine which pigment is the most apparent. Find out the names of the trees you look at.

2. What are some other changes that take place at the end or beginning of one season? Think about the trees, flowers, grass, water, animals, and sky. How do these changes affect you?

3. Think of another kind of process, such as making coffee or tea, washing clothes, applying to a university, or finding a book in the library. Think of the steps involved in this process and the factors that can influence the success of the process. For this assignment you will work in small groups. Each person in the group will have a specific task. You will have two minutes to explain the process. One of your classmates will take notes on the steps you mention and then try to retell the process. Other students will comment on how clear the explanation was. After class, you can write your description in paragraph form.

4. Find a diagram of a process in an encyclopedia or text from another class. You may use a flow chart, a graph, or a set of pictures. With a classmate, study the diagram and write one paragraph to describe the process. Be sure to include connecting expressions that show the order of the steps and the effects of each step.

Discussion Notes

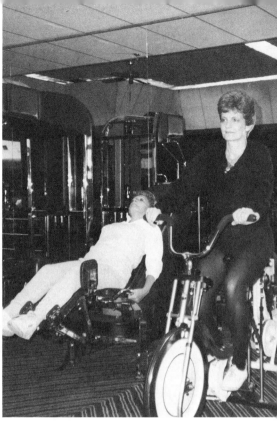

LESSON

14/ Wellness

A. Speaker

Wayne H. Osness is a professor of exercise physiology at the University of Kansas in the Department of Health, Physical Education, and Recreation. He received his doctorate from the University of Wisconsin in 1966. He has been a researcher in the area of exercise physiology, teacher at both the high school and college levels, and chairman of the Department of Health, Physical Education, and Recreation. He has written many publications and given presentations both nationally and internationally.

B. Background

In the United States today, people are aware that the way they live can affect their health. Because of this, many people try to eat food that will help them stay healthy. For example, eating many vegetables and fruit instead of a great amount of red meat can help prevent heart disease and other illnesses. People who are interested in better health also try to exercise regularly.

C. Prelistening Discussion

Think about the topic, and make a list of statements. For example, you might write, "Many Americans want to improve their health." These sentences are your ideas about what will be in the lecture. Later in the lesson, after you have listened to the lecture, look at the statements again and decide if your statements were true or false.

_____

_____

_____

_____

_____

D. Prelistening Vocabulary

Before you listen to the lecture, practice the pronunciation of the following key words with your teacher. Notice the syllable in each word with the most important stress.

General   *Read the sentence for each word. For* **synonyms**, *think of another word or other words that could replace the italicized word. For* **other forms**, *write in nouns, adjectives, or other word forms of the italicized word.*

1. disease
   (disEASE)

A *disease* is something that keeps a living being from functioning normally.

SYNONYMS: *infection, contagion*

Other forms: *diseased*

115

2. prevention
   (preVENtion)

   The *prevention* of the spread of smallpox protected the public.

   SYNONYMS: _____

   Other forms: _____

3. drastically
   (DRAStically)

   The teacher *drastically* increased the amount of homework from two pages to six.

   SYNONYMS: _____

   Other forms: _____

4. strategies
   (STRATegies)

   Politicians have *strategies* to change public opinion.

   SYNONYMS: _____

   Other forms: _____

5. heightened
   (HEIGHTened)

   He *heightened* his enjoyment of the movie by eating popcorn.

   SYNONYMS: _____

   Other forms: _____

6. trauma
   (TRAUma)

   A *trauma* can upset a person physically and emotionally.

   SYNONYMS: _____

   Other forms: _____

Field-specific *For each of the following words, read the sentence and use the context to guess the definition. Write the meaning in your own words if possible.*

7. nutrition intervention
   (nuTRItion interVENtion)

   The *nutrition intervention* stopped people from eating food that would hurt them.

   MEANING: _____

8. stress management
   (STRESS MANagement)

   Stress management reduces the amount of stress in your life.

   MEANING: _____

9. life-style choices
   (LIFE-STYLE CHOICes)

   Life-style choices give us freedom to change our lives.

   MEANING: _____

10. fitness centers
    (FITness CENters)

Fitness centers have machines to help people exercise their bodies.

MEANING: _____

E. Note-Taking Technique: 1. Recognizing Rephrasing

Many times, instead of giving the meaning of the word in a lecture, a speaker will rephrase or say the same thing in other words. For example, Osness says, ". . . those programs that relate to exercise, uh . . . appropriate exercise for given individuals. . . ." Notice that "those programs that relate to exercise" and "appropriate exercise for given individuals" mean almost the same thing. The speaker is saying this to give the listener time to understand what he is saying.

The following is a section from the lecture Osness gives about wellness. When you see a place in the talk where Osness has used paraphrasing, or said the same thing in other words, underline the original statement and place two lines below the place where he has paraphrased. Draw an arrow from the original statement to the paraphrase.

When we talk about health and wellness . . . uh . . . we immediately think about uh . . . handling problems that uh . . . that happen uh . . . in a disease nature. However, we're also concerned about prevention, and those programs that relate to exercise, uh . . . appropriate exercise for given individuals and nutritional programs to make sure that diet is sufficient, uh . . . stress management to reduce the incidence of stress in our lives, and a proper uh . . . choice of personal habits.

. . . .

Also, fortunately uh . . . our scientists have provided a greater uh . . . wealth of information uh . . . from scientific findings indicating the effect of various kinds of intervention strategies uh . . . to the end result. In other words, what can we expect if we do engage in an exercise program or in nu uh . . . ni uh . . . nutrition intervention program.

When you are able to recognize this rephrasing easily, it will help you when you take notes on a lecture. It will give you more time to write down the new information instead of writing down every idea that you hear.

F. Main Idea/Organization Check

Read through these questions or statements before you listen to the tape. As you listen to the lecture for the first time, listen for the main ideas. Circle the letter of the best answer.

This is not a note-taking exercise. You will have a chance to take notes on the material later.

1. At the beginning of the lecture, Osness discusses _____.
   a. health and wellness
   b. exercise only
   c. the cost of health care

2. Osness indicates the scientific findings on the effects of intervention strategies have resulted in _____.
   a. more expense for patients
   b. fitness centers in hospitals
   c. more hospitalization

3. When Osness discusses colleges and universities, he indicates health educators are now focusing on _____.
   a. rehabilitation
   b. helping the sick patient
   c. keeping people well

G. Note-Taking Technique: 2. Formal Outlining

In the Harris lesson, there is an example of how to formally organize an outline. You may want to look at that example on pages 8 and 9 before doing this exercise. On page 119, take notes on this lecture, and then reorganize them into a formal outline form in the space provided.

H. Note-Taking Guide Page

INFORMAL NOTES:

FORMAL OUTLINE:

Lesson 14

I. Review Strategy: Starring Important Information

When students study, they will many times review their notes to look for important information that might be on a test. This helps them decide how to organize their study time more effectively. Look at your formal outline and place a star (*) to the left of any information that you think is especially important.

[◎◎] J. Feature of the Lecture: Academic Phrasing

When professors in universities give a lecture, they speak differently than when they talk to their families or friends. They use more formal language and phrases. For example, Osness says, "There's a strong concern today in our society for health and wellness uh . . . among those of us in the United States and around the world." This could be said in a simpler way: "People all around the world are worried today about health and wellness."

Turn to the script for Osness on page 158 and follow the directions given.

K. Comprehension Exercise: True/False

Use your notes to decide whether each of the following statements is *true* or *false*. If the statement is *false*, underline the information that is incorrect. Change this information so that the statement will be true, according to the lecture. Circle *T* for true and *F* for false.

1. *T* *F* Prevention programs only teach appropriate exercises for individuals.

2. *T* *F* Stress management increases the incidence of stress in our lives.

3. *T* *F* The cost of health care in the United States is increasing.

4. *T* *F* Fifteen percent of the illnesses that we experience today can be avoided by having good life-styles.

5. *T* *F* College programs need to also teach wellness concepts.

Turn back to page 115 and look at the statements you wrote about the lecture. Decide if they were true or false.

L. Comprehension Exercise: Short Essay

Choose one of the following topics. Write a paragraph using information from your notes.

1. Describe the health and wellness concerns of the next decade, according to Osness.
2. Osness mentions several ways to reduce health care costs. List them and tell whether you agree with these ideas.

M. Discussion or Written Assignments

1. Do you follow an exercise program?
2. Is health care expensive? Give some specific examples.
3. Do most countries have national health care? If so, how is it paid for and how does it work? What are the advantages and disadvantages of such a system?

120

4. What do you think is the best form of stress management?

5. Which food do you regularly eat in order to stay healthy?

6. Read an article about a health-related topic, and either write a report or report orally to the class.

Discussion Notes

A. Speaker

David E. Shulenburger is a professor of business and associate vice-chancellor of academic affairs at the University of Kansas. He has a doctorate in labor and industrial relations from the University of Illinois. His research areas have included wage determination and the impacts of wage and price controls. He serves on the board of the Center for International Programs at the University of Kansas.

B. Background

Anyone who travels to another country knows that when we change our money to that of another country, we have trouble understanding what it is worth. This lecture explains the 1944 international agreement on the value of money and how the agreement and changes in the agreement affected the value of each country's money.

C. Prereading

International monetary fund (IMF) is an organization of more than 145 member nations that works to establish an efficient system of international payments and trade. It seeks to help its members achieve rapid economic growth, a high level of employment, and improved standards of living. The IMF serves as an agency for consultation on world monetary and debt problems. Its members cooperate to maintain orderly exchange arrangements between nations.

The IMF was established after the Bretton Woods Conference of 1944. It began operating in 1947 with a fund of $9 billion in gold and currency, of which the United States contributed about a third. The IMF uses the fund to help members meet problems regarding balance of payments. In 1969, the IMF created a type of reserve assets called Special Drawing Rights (SDRs) to supplement international reserves of gold and currencies. By the early 1980s the IMF had assets of about $50 billion.

The IMF is a specialized agency of the United Nations. The agency is closely connected with the World Bank. A nation must be a member of the IMF before it can belong to the bank. The IMF has headquarters at 19th and H Streets NW, Washington, DC 20431.

From *The World Book Encyclopedia.* © 1989 World Book, Inc.

After reading the passage about the International Monetary Fund, answer the following questions about it, and then discuss your answers with your teacher.

1. How many member nations does the International Monetary Fund have?
2. What is the organization's main focus?
3. What are the three ways that the IMF seeks to help its members?
4. When was the IMF established?
5. What did the IMF create in 1969 to supplement international reserves of gold and currencies?
6. What well-known organizations is the IMF closely associated with?

D. Prelistening Discussion

1. Compare the value of one unit of currency from another country with that of the U.S. dollar.
2. Has this value changed in recent years? Why?
3. What happens to trade between countries when inflation rates go up?

E. Prelistening Vocabulary

Before you listen to the lecture, practice the pronunciation of the following key words with your teacher. Notice the syllable in each word with the most important stress.

General   *Read the sentence for each word. For* **synonyms**, *think of another word or other words that could replace the italicized word. For* **other forms**, *write in nouns, adjectives, or other word forms of the italicized word.*

1. relationship
   (reLAtionship)

   There is a *relationship* between how much a person studies and the grade he or she receives.

   SYNONYMS: *association, interdependence*

   Other forms: *relate, related, relating*

2. hence
   (HENCE)

   He didn't do the work; *hence*, he did not get paid.

   SYNONYMS: _____

   Other forms: _____

3. designed
   (deSIGNED)

   That test was *designed* to learn how much grammar the student understood.

   SYNONYMS: _____

   Other forms: _____

4. facilitate
   (faCILitate)

   I hope this English class will *facilitate* your adjustment to a university.

   SYNONYMS: _____

   Other forms: _____

5. initial
   (inItial)

   My *initial* impression of the man was not a good one, but I have changed my mind about him.

   SYNONYMS: _____

   Other forms: _____

6. currency
   (CURrency)

   The *currency* of each country usually consists of coins and paper money.

   SYNONYMS: _____

   Other forms: _____

7. essentially
   (esSENtially)

   Essentially, the only thing he wanted was to be loved.

   SYNONYMS: _____

   Other forms: _____

8. sensible
   (SENsible)

   It is a *sensible* idea to always carry an umbrella on cloudy days.

   SYNONYMS: _____

   Other forms:

9. destruction
   (deSTRUCtion)

   The earthquake caused the total *destruction* of the city.

   SYNONYMS: _____

   Other forms: _____

10. inflation
    (inFLAtion)

    Because of *inflation*, everything we buy costs much more than it did last year.

    SYNONYMS: _____

    Other forms: _____

11. substantially
    (subSTANtially)

    At his new job, he made *substantially* more money.

    SYNONYMS: _____

    Other forms: _____

12. reaction
    (reACtion)

    The *reaction* of the two chemicals was surprising; when we mixed them there was smoke.

    SYNONYMS: _____

    Other forms: _____

13. convert
    (conVERT)

    When you travel to another country, you must *convert* your money to the currency of that country.

    SYNONYMS: _____

    Other forms: _____

14. misalignment
    (misaLIGNment)

    There is a *misalignment* in the wheels; they are not even.

    SYNONYMS: _____

Other forms: _____

15. competitively
    (comPETitively)

Professional athletes always want to win; they do everything *competitively*.

SYNONYMS: _____

Other forms: _____

16. unpredictable
    (unpreDICTable)

He never does the same thing twice; he is *unpredictable*.

SYNONYMS: _____

Other forms: _____

Field-specific   *For each of the following words, read the sentence and use the context to guess the definition. Write the meaning in your own words if possible.*

17. International Monetary
    Fund
    (interNAtional MONetary
    FUND)

The *International Monetary Fund* controlled the value of money for many years.

MEANING: _____

18. key currencies
    (KEY CURrencies)

A *key currency* is one that is very important to the world economy.

MEANING: _____

19. trade
    (TRADE)

Trade is important to both countries because they can exchange goods.

MEANING: _____

20. purchasing power
    parity
    (PURchasing POWer
    PARity)

When you have *purchasing power parity*, your trade with other countries is equal.

MEANING: _____

21. differential inflation
    rates
    (differENtial inFLAtion
    RATES)

With the *differential inflation rates*, I can't buy as much in your country as before.

MEANING: _____

22. destabilizing
    (deSTAbilizing)

Spending too much money has a *destabilizing* effect on your budget.

MEANING: _____

23. depression
    (dePRESsion)

When there was a *depression* in the country, people had trouble finding work.

MEANING: _____

24. devalue
    (deVALue)

When the money was *devalued*, it took more of it to buy anything.

MEANING: _____

25. float
    (FLOAT)

When they allowed the money to *float*, no one knew what would happen.

MEANING: _____

F. Note-Taking Technique: Using Graphs to Show Processes

In several other lessons, you have used diagrams for your notes. In this lecture, an economic process is described in a graph form. This condenses a great deal of material in a small area. This could be included along with other notes on the lecture to help include more information and make it easier to review for a test.

G. Main Idea/Organization Check

Read through these questions or statements before you listen to the tape. As you listen to the lecture for the first time, listen for the main ideas. Circle the letter of the best answer.

This is not a note-taking exercise. You will have a chance to take notes on the material later.

1. At the beginning of his lecture, Shulenburger describes _____ of the International Monetary Fund in 1944.
   a. only the nations
   b. the basic organization
   c. key currencies

2. Later in the lecture, Shulenburger describes what occurred when _____.
   a. purchasing power parity developed
   b. differential inflation rates developed
   c. nations failed to cooperate

3. At the end of his lecture, Shulenburger describes what _____ the change in U.S. policy in the early 1970s.
   a. caused
   b. helped prevent
   c. resulted from

H. Note-Taking Guide Page

As you listen to the tape, try to fill in the information on page 128. This will help you develop the skills to listen for chronological information in other lectures.

Lesson 15

H. Note-Taking Guide Page

Date		Effect on Currency Rate
		agreement ___currencies based on _____; then on one another
1944 - 1971	Problems	↓ devaluing money
	Nixon	

Fig. 15-1 International Monetary Fund

I. Review Strategy: Predicting Exam Questions

In the Haack lesson on page 26, you practiced predicting exam questions. To the left of your notes that you have just taken on page 128, write in any question you think could be on a test.

⊗⊗ J. Feature of the Lecture: Using the Passive

The Shulenburger lesson contains many passive structures such as *was defined* and *thus being defined*. The passive construction is often used to describe past situations objectively.

Turn to the script for Shulenburger on page 160 and follow the directions given.

K. Comprehension Exercise: True/False

Use your notes to decide whether each of the following statements is *true* or *false*. If the statement is *false*, underline the information that is incorrect. Change this information so that the statement will be true, according to the lecture. Circle *T* for true and *F* for false.

1. *T* *F*   In 1948, the International Monetary Fund was formed.

2. *T* *F*   The United States, France, and Germany defined their currencies as key currencies.

3. *T* *F*   A key currency meant that the value of their currency was defined in terms of gold.

4. *T* *F*   The remaining countries of the noncommunist world defined their currencies in terms of each other.

5. *T* *F*   Following 1944, differential inflation rates occurred among the countries that agreed to be part of the International Monetary Fund system.

6. *T* *F*   Because of the misalignment among countries, some countries competitively devalued their currencies.

7. *T* *F*   In 1961, Richard Nixon abandoned the International Monetary Fund's fixed rate exchange system.

L. Comprehension Exercise: Short Essay

Choose one or two of the following topics. For each one, write a paragraph using information from your notes.

1. What was the original purpose of the International Monetary Fund?
2. Was the original purpose effective? Why or why not?
3. What events were triggered by the differential inflation rates after 1944? Describe the cycle.

M. Discussion or Written Assignments

1. Check with a bank to see the exchange rates for several currencies.

2. How can countries facilitate trade these days?

3. Should governments impose control on imports and exports?

4. Should we only buy products that are made in our own countries? Why or why not?

5. Find an article about a trade issue or agreement and report to the class about it.

Discussion Notes

Introduction to Scripts

*The scripts that follow are really **transcripts** of each of the short lectures. You will notice some unusual sentences. Sometimes the speakers hesitate in order to think or to give the listener time to understand their ideas. For these hesitations, you will see <u>uh</u> or <u>. . . .</u> **These are the exact words of the speakers**. You may notice some mistakes in grammar or some incomplete sentences. This is typical of spoken English. Written English is more formal.*

To help you analyze the features of each speaker's lecture, there are exercises with each script. The scripts are double-spaced so that you can complete the exercises.

Script for Lesson 1

SPREADSHEETS
Herb Harris

As you listen to the tape again, listen for the phrases that are repeated in exactly the same way or somewhat differently. Underline the phrase when it is first used, and underline the phrase twice when it is repeated. Then draw an arrow to the first phrase you underlined. Harris also uses linking expressions to connect his ideas. Circle the linking expressions as you hear them.

I would like to talk about the concept of spreadsheets on microcomputers. Spreadsheets on microcomputers are very important in the development of the use of microcomputers. They in fact are a watershed in the use of microcomputers.

With the development of spreadsheets, uh . . . the business community found a use for microcomputers and since they found a use, they bought a lot   5
of them, and when they bought a lot of them, the microcomputer revolution really began. So the microcomputer revolution is based upon the development of the spreadsheet.

The spreadsheet in fact was developed by two people at M.I.T., and people immediately recognized the usefulness of it. In its most elementary   10
form, the spreadseet . . . sheet is just a matrix of rows and columns. In each cell, three types of information can be stored. First, there is label information or textual information. Typically, you would use this kind of cell to label a row or a column. For example, in a budget you could label costs or expenditures or types of costs, types of expenditures. Second, uh . . . in a cell you can   15
have a number. This number uh . . . can be monetary, it could be a date, it can be a floating point number or an integer number. Finally, in each cell, you can store a formula. And the formula can in fact involve other she . . . other cells in the sheet itself, so that the sh . . . the sheet can be dynamic. When you change one cell, if that cell is involved in formulas, values in all the other   20
cells will change automatically. Now, for example, when you're doing a budget and you want to see what changing one variable will do to the bottom line, you can change that . . . that variable and all other values in the sheet are recalculated automatically a . . . allowing you to see what the effect of changing that variable will be. This dynamism uh . . . this automatic and immediate   25
dynamism in playing "what if" games is one of things that sold the business community on using spreadsheets, especially for budgets.

Script for Lesson 2

DEMOGRAPHICS OF INTERNATIONAL STUDENTS IN THE UNITED STATES
Clark Coan

As you listen to the tape again, listen for the phrases that indicate a list or additional information will follow. Underline the phrases.

Some . . . people would probably like to know some of the demographics about uh . . . study in the United States. Our uh . . . statistics nationally show that there are approximately 342,000 foreign students studying in the United States including some 25,000 in Intensive English programs. The countries that right now send the most students here are Taiwan, Malaysia which interestingly   5
enough has gone up 20 percent from the previous year, Nigeria and Iran which both have gone down. The Republic of Korea having gone up and as would uh . . . be uh . . . guessed, Venezuela has gone down.

It might be appropriate to give a little bit of information about uh . . . fields of study uh . . . People think that uh . . . all foreign students are just   10
in one or two fields and that's somewhat true but engineering would be the largest, business management uh . . . math and science that has taken an increase from previous years, social sciences, fine arts, health sciences, humanities, education in that order.

The uh . . . uh . . . types of funding which students have — personal and   15
family funding has always been the prime source followed by home government, home university, U.S. government, foreign private sponsors, and uh . . . U.S. universities. Seventy percent of the foreign students studying in the United States at the present time are male uh . . . 80 percent single uh . . . 83½ percent hold the student visa, which sounds appropriate. Almost 88 per-   20
cent of the students are in four-year schools and 65 percent of those are in public or state universities. uh . . . The graduate programs seem to be making a significant impact, and it might be interesting to know that 10 percent of graduate enrollment in the United States is foreign . . . . . . uh . . . compared to only 2.7 percent of all U.S. student population being foreign. So uh . . . it   25
seems rather important.

Also should mention that when we are talking about numbers, that in Intensive English programs the countries of origin change. Japan is the first, the Republic of Korea, followed by Saudi Arabia, and Indonesia as the top ones. The . . . some of the significant changes that have occurred in the past *30* few years uh . . . I believe students might think that uh . . . we have no Europeans at universities, but actually the numbers of Europeans uh . . . have gone up. Proportionately no, but have stayed about the same because we've had such increases in students from the countries I've mentioned. Particularly from Southeast and South Asia. But uh . . . uh . . . for example at our university *35* we have more Europeans now than we've ever had, but uh . . . proportionately that wouldn't work, that wouldn't be true.

Script for Lesson 3

PHYSIOLOGICAL EFFECTS OF MUSIC

Paul Haack

As you listen to the tape again, listen for examples of synonyms that Haack joins by the words or *and* that is. *Underline the first word in the pair and circle the second.*

Music functions in many ways, and one of the ways it communicates or affects us seems to be in the stimulative-sedative dimension. That is, certain types of music seem to stimulate us, energize us by raising our heartbeats, our blood flow rates, our blood pressure, galvanic skin response and other measurable aspects of our being. Other types of music tend to sedate us or calm us   5
by lowering our blood flow rate and our heartbeat rate and so on.

Musical aspects that seem to be stimulative are disjunct or jumpy melodies . . . um . . . irregular harmonies, that is, harmonies that don't flow the way we anticipate them at times and have dissonances in them. And irregular rhythms that don't just flow consistently and repeatedly. Raising the tempo   10
rate, in that is increasing the tempo, can be stimulative whether it's done gradually or suddenly. And changing dynamics can be stimulative. That is, sudden accents or delayed gradual crescendos — increasing loudness gradually.

The reverse or the opposite tends to be sedative. Melodies that are very uh . . . smooth flowing. Harmonies that present us with the expected changes.   15
Rhythms that are repetitive. Tempos that are constant and dynamics that uh . . . don't vary a great deal. These things tend to sedate us, make us more calm, relaxed.

However, the research findings on this topic remain rather inconclusive and certainly more information is needed, especially on the cross-cultural effects of   20
music.

Script for Lesson 4

AN ELECTRIC FIELD
Gordon G. Wiseman

In lines 1 to 5, circle the key words that you hear Wiseman emphasize.

(Quantities) in in the (physical) sciences, in (physics) in particular, are often defined in terms of operations that . . . uh . . . one preform, performs in order to actually m . . . measure that quantity. Uh . . . these kinds of definitions are called operational . . . uh . . . definitions, and I'll pick an example of the definition of an electric field to illustrate uh . . . this point. 5

*In the next section, Wiseman hesitates and uses some fillers such as **uh** in his explanation. Draw a light pencil line through these fillers and concentrate on the main points as you listen.*

Let me describe the operations, in ~~of~~ . . . ~~uh~~ . . . not necessarily in order but the necessary operations. The first one would be to place a test charge, and that could be uh . . . real or imagin . . . uh . . . imagi . . . uh . . . imaginary, at the point at which you want the electric field, and you would write down the symbol q . . . uh for that uh test charge, and it is always . . . uh a positive in 10 sign rather than a negative. The second uh part of the operation uh would be to . . . uh measure or calculate if you wish, the force uh uh given by the symbol F that is exerted on that charge by the the electric field. The third part of that operation, or the third operation, is to divide that force F by q, the charge, in order to get the answer which will will be designated by the symbol E. 15

In the last section, circle the key words as you did in the first section.

Now there are some very (definite) (cautions) about this uh . . . procedure. Uh . . . first is that the force F is a vector, rather than a ordinary quantity. By that I mean it has direction as well as magnitude, and so the electric field that you come up with is a . . . uh is a vector quantity. The second precaution is that the small test charge, . . . this positive small charge that you select, 20 uh . . . should be very, very small so that uh its presence does not cause any shift in the source of the electric field. And so we have the definition then of the electric field as a ratio of force to charge and . . . uh . . . th . . . that electric field is a vector measured in newtons per coulomb.

Script for Lesson 5

TJI WARA: A HEADCREST MASK

Robert T. Soppelsa

For Soppelsa's introduction (lines 1 to 9), circle the key words as he stresses them. Notice how he pauses slightly after these key words. What word introduces a list in this section? _____

This object is (called) a (tji wara.) It's a (headcrest) (mask) from the Bamana of the grasslands in Mali in West Africa. Uh, a mask is part of masquerade and as we see them in Western museums, in museums in Europe and the United States, they are incomplete as works of art. Uh . . . masquerade is a very complex art form involving a costume, a sculpture, that is the mask, move-   *5* ment, song, the response of the audience, the location, the time of year, and a number of other things that can't be duplicated in Western culture. However, the mask itself, the headcrest itself, is interesting as a piece of art and tells us a lot about the culture that produced it.

What is the main idea of the next section? As you hear a pause in Soppelsa's voice, draw a slash (/) to mark the phrase.

*Tji wara/*in Bamana/means cultivator beast,/or beast/that cultivates./There   *10* is a Bamana myth/that says the antelope taught man how to farm by running across the fields, digging up the soil with its hooves. Uh . . . here, we see a mother antelope, with a baby antelope on its back. Antelopes, of course, don't carry their babies around like this. They couldn't, the baby's hooves would cut the mother's back. Thus, the antelope is represented anthropomorphically. It is   *15* represented like a human being in that the mother carries baby on back like human mothers carry their babies on backs.

In lines 18 to 30, you hear information about the male and female antelope dancers. Listen for the sentence patterns that describe each one. Go back to your notes and see if you got all the characteristics for each one.

When tji wara are danced, they are danced in pairs, with a male and a female, ideally like humans organize themselves in society and the female, as the ideal human female mother would have, carries the baby on the back. Here   *20* we have the mother with a male baby. We can identify the baby as a male because he has a complex carved mane whereas the mother has no mane at all.

138

The . . . uh, male antelope would ha . . . would be large like the female antelope is here, like the mother antelope is here and he would have a complex carved mane as well. Note also that the mother antelope has very human-looking ears which wear earrings, which of course antelopes don't do either, and that she has a ring through her nose which again represents her anthropomorphically in that she is represented with pierced septum. Her face is shaped like a human face. But otherwise, she looks like an antelope and very . . . is very elegant in line, like the antelope as it runs across the savannah.

In the following section, Soppelsa describes the young men's organization and the use of the masquerade. In lines 31 to 42, notice the parallel sentences. What does he repeat in order to list the occasions for the dances?

Now of course, antelopes don't cultivate. However, *tji wara* means not only the cultivator beast but it also is the name of the young men's organization in Bamana society, for young men between ages of about eighteen and twenty-five. This is the age at which young men come into adulthood, they marry, they begin to farm as adult males, and begin to have children. Thus, tji wara is the ideal family unit as well as this . . . pair of antelopes and tji wara as an organization is a device that prepares young Bamana men for their roles in adult . . . uh . . . economic life. Therefore, the masquerade is more than just an object of art. They don't put them in museums in Africa. They, at harvests, at funerals, and at initiation ceremonies, they bring them out and they dance wearing, young men dance, wearing these masks in order to reinforce in one another the important notions of adulthood and adult life.

In lines 43 to 52, notice how Soppelsa repeats information from his introduction. Which lines give you more information for the lists you made in your notes?

And the mask is only one part of this. As I said, there is a song, there are songs that are sung . . . uh . . . with this masquerade, the masks themselves speak and the audience responds to the masks. There is . . . uh . . . the location, the masks are danced in the fields where the cultivation will, or is, going to take place. There are the costumes of the masks. The mas . . . uh . . . the masqueraders themselves dance on their feet and hold canes in their two hands, so that they, in fact, have four feet. Like the antelopes, have four feet. And the female mask dances with a great deal of grace and lithesomeness in its movement, and the male mask dances with much more energy and aggressiveness in its movements.

25

30

35

40

45

50

139

In the conclusion, mark the phrases with a slash. Listen for the pauses in his voice. Notice how Soppelsa's voice drops for the last phrase.

So we see these masks in museums as beautiful objects themselves which are worn with age and shiny from being touched with . . . uh, by human hands, but they are only one tiny part of a complex and beautiful and very 55 interesting art form, that we need to appreciate if we are to ever appreciate African art in its cultural context and in its entirety.

Script for Lesson 6

THE SLOPE OF A LINE
Philip Montgomery

For the first section of Montgomery's explanation, listen for the focus cues that connect old information to new information. Put a box around these expressions.

Today, I wanna talk about the slope of a line. The slope of a line is a number which is attached to a line and gives some indication of . . . the steepness of the line in the direction in which it goes. It's obtained in the following way. Draw any line in any — in any position and pick two points on the line. Call one of the points P and the second point Q. (drawing noise) From the point P draw a horizontal line. From the point Q draw a vertical line, and draw the vertical line in such a way eh that it will meet the horizontal line, and let's call the point where they meet R. You should then have a right angle triangle with the right angle at the point R and . . . the hypotenuse of the of the right angle triangle being the line segment between P and Q . . . . . . Now, take the distance from P to R and call that the run. Take the distance from Q to R and call that the rise.

Continue to mark the focus cues in the next section. In lines 13 to 23, listen for the contrastive stress. Circle the words that Montgomery contrasts. Put a matching number next to each item in the pair. What is the formula for slope? _____

Now, in this we have to remember to take what are called signed distances, that is a uh . . . uh . . . distance can be negative. The distances are measured in the following way. For the horizontal lines if you'd measure to the right, you're measuring positively. If you measure to the left, you should be measuring negatively. For the vertical line, a line which goes up is measured in the positive direction, and a line which goes down is measured in the negative direction. O.K. So we now have a uh triangle. We have the legs of the triangle being the line segment from P to R which we have called the run and the line segment from Q to R which we have called the rise. The slope is given by the ratio of the signed distance, the rise, divided by the signed distance, the run.

In this last section, listen for how Montgomery summarizes the differences in slopes of lines. He will mention vertical lines, horizontal lines, and positive and negative slopes. Listen to the way Montgomery's voice falls at the end of each contrast. Put a box around each contrast.

Now this thing will uh . . . always be defined except for one particular case, and that is, when the line L that you drew, or given is a vertical line. So a vertical line has no slope. If you have a horizontal line, where the rise is zero, then you have slope is equal to zero. So, a vertical line and a horizontal line in some sense are uh . . . opposites of one another. A vertical line has a lot of rise and no run and doesn't have a slope. A horizontal line has a no rise and a lot of run and has a zero slope. For everything else the . . . the number M will give an indication of steepness and it will also be positive or negative. Positive slopes will be . . . correspond to lines which go from the bottom left to the top right, and negative slopes will be lines which go from the top left to the bottom right. In other words, fall. Uh . . . positive slopes are lines which run. The larger the slope is, the steeper the line is. This is also true for negative slopes if you're uh . . . wh- take the absolute value of the slope to be an indication of the steepness.

25

30

35

Script for Lesson 7

ADJUSTMENT OF STUDENTS (PART A)

Diane McDermott

As you listen to the tape again, listen for the words or phrases that signal to the listener that the speaker is beginning a new topic. Underline the words or phrases.

I'm going to speak about student adjustment problems, and people come to the University Counseling Center uh . . . oftentimes with the very kind of student adjustment problems that I'm going to be speaking about. And I see probably . . . oh probably five or ten people a week with these very kinds of things. And and I'm going to give a little thought to how they come about and 5 what they are.

To begin with, uh . . . when people first come to the university, to a university or college, they are usually, assuming that they're coming at the usual age of 17 or 18 years old, they're usually in the developmental period in which they're right in the very heart of forming their own identity, their own 10 sense of self. And they're they're also in a period of having to and . . . and wanting to break away from their family group, their . . . their parents and their . . . their siblings, in other words, they're trying to form their own iden- tity, to uh . . . differentiate who they are from who they've always thought they were as part of their family. 15

But when they come to the university, they have a whole lot, suddenly to have a whole lot of freedom and a whole lot of different kinds of decisions that they have to . . . to make. One of the first things that they have to do of course is to decide what kind of a living unit they're going to . . . to live in, and there are a lot of options that they have, such as apartments, or uh . . . 20 residence halls, or scholarship halls, or or even what kind of a residence hall.

So that right off the bat is the first decision, 'course that's often made right in the . . . in the home still because it has to be made before they get here. But once they get here, you know, then they have forms to fill out where they have to declare a major or pick some subject area and that's going to . . . 25 that's uh . . . sometimes that's a real overwhelming decision right off the bat. They have uh . . . things that they have to be responsible for, in their living

143

situation that they may not have been responsible for before like what kind of food they're gonna eat, are they gonna eat a lot of junk food? Are they going to uh . . . be able to maintain a good . . . some good health habits while *30* they're here, and for a lot of kids or a lot of young people, that's pretty new experience. They don't have Mom over . . . overseeing anymore what they put in their bodies or on their bodies or washing the clothes, or whatever and that's that's kind of im . . . important, although I don't think most students actually have major problems with that, I . . . I bring it out because it's . . . it's some- *35* thing that they do have to deal with oftentimes for the first time on their own.

Script for Lesson 8

ADJUSTMENT OF STUDENTS (PART B)
Diane McDermott

As you listen to the tape again, listen for the words or phrases that signal to the listener that the speaker is beginning a new topic. Underline the words or phrases.

Uh . . . actually some of the major things that hit are there is no longer a requirement to go to class. They uh . . . they can miss class, they can sleep through if they want to, they can um . . . they can just blow it off. Um . . . they don't have to study. And lots of people come in in there they uh . . . around midterm time in their freshman year, the first semester of their fresh-   *5* man year and they're flunking. And they're flunking because they really haven't gone to class and they really haven't studied and it's caught up with them and they really have to learn how to deal with that.

And so those are those are real important decisions and then there are some other kinds of decisions that uh . . . they have to make, and very difficult   *10* ones. For example, using alcohol or other kinds of drugs and as much as we would like to say that drugs are illegal on a college campus, the fact of the matter is that they are around, all over the place and there's a tremendous amount of pressure on young people to start drinking, to go to beer parties or other kinds of things, and for a student who's been pretty sheltered, or who   *15* hasn't learned to, who hasn't reached a maturity level where those things can be dealt with, they can be very devastating.

Another decision has to be made is the decision about sex . . . because it nobody is . . . is really looking over your shoulder anymore about what time you come in, at night, or who you have in the re- . . . who you have in your   *20* dorm room, quite frankly. And those the opportunities are there, and if a person isn't emotionally prepared for them in the family or whatever they've come from, you know, before they get here, if they're not emotionally pre-pared, those things can be absolutely overwhelming, and students come in having . . . either realizing that they need help in making these decisions, and   *25* that's great because then they're coming in.

Going to a counselor when you know that you've got some important decisions to make and you're not sure how you can make them, that's preventative and that's great. Too often students come in having already made wrong decisions, de- de-decisions that were wrong for them, there aren't necessarily *30* wrong decisions, but there are ones that're are wrong for some people and they'll come in having . . . wanting to work with a counselor in mopping it up. Um . . . so these are . . . I think these are probably the major problems in student adjustment that occur, that we see here in the Counseling Center.

Script for Lesson 9
PETROLEUM FORMATION
Lawrence L. Brady

As you listen to the tape again, listen for the word that is defined and then listen for the definition. Underline the word with one line and the definition with two lines. Then draw an arrow from the definition to the word it defines.

Today I wanna talk about petroleum and geology. There are five important factors when we think about the occurrence and why we have petroleum. There's source rock which is the rock in which the organic material or the petroleum is actually derived, the reservoir rock which by the process of migration carries the uh . . . oil from the source rock to another mechanism called the trap. The trap then is where the petroleum accumulates and where we presently would obtain by oil wells the material. Within that trap though, in order to contain the petroleum we have what we call the seal.

Well, let's let's briefly talk about each of these. The source rock is composed of clays, muds, salt water we believe in most cases it's been marine derived, and the large amount of organic material from plants and animals that accumulated in that is the basis for the production of the petroleum. The petroleum then is squeezed from this rock with heat and pressure over time. This material then migrates or we're we're in the process of migration in a reservoir rock or a more porous rock that allows the fluids to flow through this rock and while it's flowin' through this rock it may encounter something we call the trap. This may be either a structure which is a bending of the rocks such as uh . . . a . . . salt dome area in the Gulf Coast of the U.S. It can be uh two terms geologists use—a dome, an anticline. The dome would be approximate bending of the same amount in each direction or . . . s . . . anticline would be stronger bending in one direction and a longer bending in the other direction. Well, this forms the trap in which the the migrating fluids going through the reservoir rock encounter this the buoyancy of the oil goes higher into the trap, and it is then held there particularly if you have a seal. And what a seal is is a a rock that will not allow the oil to migrate through it. In other words, if the trap has a seal over the top of the reservoir rock, we have the oil in the reservoir rock that's held by the seal and totally within this structure or the trap that occurs there. There are, there is another well-known trappin' . . . mes . . .

mechanism called the stratigraphic trap. And in a stratigraphic trap two exam- *30*
ples would be an ancient sandstone river uh . . . channel perhaps an ancient
uh . . . carbonate reef. And these, these form the basis then for the oil to
migrate into this and to be trapped within this very porous zone by the seal
that overlies it.

So just reemphasizin' these points, we have the source rock, the migration,
the reservoir rock, the trap, and the seal within the trap. Geologists will drill *35*
into this trap to get the oil out. If we have a high gas content we can get a
gusher. But in most cases, as you'll see from oil wells in the middle part of
the United States, and a good part of the world, they have to be removed by
pumping. So you can see, scien . . . tific work over time has shown that the
source rocks are important and all of these other factors that we just covered *40*
lead to the important things that we know today in geology and petroleum.
Thanks.

Script for Lesson 10

GAME THEORY AND MICROECONOMICS

Elaine Bennett

In the first section, listen for information that Bennett rephrases. When you hear something a second time, circle the phrase and put a line under the earlier reference.

One can think of economics as being a subdiscipline of game theory or perhaps even a tool to be used um in economics, but actually the perspective of game theory and economics, microeconomics, are actually s . . . somewhat different. Think about microeconomics as the decision-making problem of a single individual faced with an uncertain world. Perhaps, think of uh . . . of . . . um certain economic decisions, like, how do you spend your allowance on uh beer, pizza, and the other commodities important to health and happiness. Think of um optimal decision making on whether to drill for an oil field or not. These are all economic questions which you'll find in microeconomic courses. The view is that there is a single individual who is trying to make a decision, to maximize his utility or something, taking all the rest of the world as given. For example, if you don't know whether it's going to rain or not, you get the probabilities of rain or sunshine and you put them into your computations. If you don't know whether your boss is going to fire you or not, you make probability estimates on those things and take those into account.

Um but, game theory, and this is where game theory is different, in game theory you focus, again everyone's assumed to be rational people making the best decisions they can, but you take into account the fact that people interact with other people.

*For the rest of the lecture, circle the expressions that signal conditionals. Include words and phrases such as **if** and **it would be**. Listen for the contrastive stress, too.*

For example, think about um the, suppose there were only two grocery stores in Lawrence serving a particular neighborhood. Then, the microeconomic view, for example, would be that to, one store's manager might take into account the fact that the other store's manager may charge a high price for coffee or a low price of coffee. And if he doesn't know what the other manager'll

do, he'd have to make a probability estimate and act accordingly. However, if *25*
you take a game theoretic approach to it, one would understand that the people
interact strategically, that is, what one store manager does will affect the —
what the other store manager ought to do, but what also he does affects what
the other store manager can do and ought to do. Game theory differs from uh
most of microeconomic theory in that you're focused on the strategic interac- *30*
tion of the individuals.

So, some examples of where game theory has been used in the past, well
one example is in industrial organization, again where there is various businesses or uh firms competing with each other over a market. It has also been
used to study war games. For example, if you have a battleship and I have a *35*
battleship, where you send your battleship will affect where I should send
mine, but where I send mine affects where you should send yours and the
optimal strategy then . . . involves understanding the strategic situation for both
individuals.

Thus, game theory is sometimes used as a tool in economics but presents *40*
a different perspective on how you view people and in . . . and their interac-
tions, microeconomics theory often considering a single individual and their
decision making, game theory considering the strategic interaction of people in
their decision making.

Script for Lesson 11

AUTOMATIC FEEDBACK CONTROL SYSTEMS

James R. Rowland

In lines 1 to 10, listen for the repetitions of key words. Underline the first mention of a word, and then draw a circle around the repetition.

Automatic feedback control systems are used in many different fields of engineering. I'd like to talk a little bit about what feedback control means. The term *feedback* is defined as the use of the system output to modify or change its input for the purposes of control. The dynamic system or process that we're trying to control is called the *plant*. You may think this comes from "chemical 5 processing plant" and perhaps it does because that's one of the typical applications that one would encounter. But the term *plant* can be much more general because we would be using it to describe, for example, an aircraft control system, aircraft to be controlled, uh . . . spacecraft system, or any of a number of different type of applications of that nature. 10

In lines 11 to 19, notice the contrastive stress in the description. Draw arrows between the items he contrasts. Use a pencil.

With feedback, you'd have what's called a *closed-loop system*. I would contrast this with an *open-loop* system. With an open-loop system, I would have simply the plant and some type of open-loop controller which would be telling the plant what to do. This would be based on some kind of a uh . . . preassigned . . . uh . . . set of operations for it to work on. On the 15 other hand, a closed-loop system would have, not only the plant and the controller, but it it would also have one or more sensors that could be used to determine what those variables are that one would need to feed back, and hence control.

In lines 20 to 38, listen for the parallel structures and the intonation Rowland uses. Underline the parallel structures.

The advantages of an open-loop system are primarily . . . its simplicity, its 20 lower cost, and its lower weight. I would use such systems in cases where only known inputs are applied and the plant parameters are well defined. Examples are toasters, electric fans, home lighting systems, and lawn sprinklers. Uh . . .

all of these systems operate under preset conditions without taking into account the actual output. The toaster operates for a fixed amount of time, the electric fan has a set motor speed, and the lights and sprinklers operate at set conditions until someone turns them off or they're turned off by timing mechanisms. It may be that the results from open-loop systems are suitable enough to preclude a need for more . . . elaborate or more refined closed-loop operations. And if that's the case, then I certainly wouldn't go to the extra expense or the extra. . . uh complications of using a closed-loop system.

On the other hand, there are advantages of a closed-loop system. And these are primarily the improved performance in the presence of unknown disturbance inputs or unknown system parameters. In addition, the output response of a properly designed closed-loop system is less sensitive to these disturbances and variations. Uh . . . examples are . . . include . . . uh . . . tracking system, a rudder control of a ship, . . . uh . . . home heating and air conditioning systems, and building elevators.

In this last section, listen for Rowland's rhetorical question. Circle the question that he answers himself.

Now I'd like for the students in the classroom before me to perhaps suggest some systems that they think may either be open-loop or closed-loop and then tell me which ones those are. Oh, here's one over here . . . An automatic electric clothes dryer . . . Okay, what are you gonna classify that? Is it closed-loop or open-loop? You're going to say it's closed-loop. Well that would be true if it had an electronic sensor that determines the moisture content of the clothes and shuts its off . . . itself off when they're dry, but if it's one that's based on the usual timing mechanism, then that would be open-loop. Uh . . . Manufacturers like to use the word *automatic* to . . . uh . . . encourage customers to buy their product, but it's not always automatic.

Script for Lesson 12

A REVOLUTION IN GARDENING

Judith K. Major

As you listen to the information about French gardens, notice how Major's intonation indicates a list. For each characteristic, write a number above it (1, 2, etc.). On the last word of each phrase used for a characteristic, draw a rising arrow to show that her voice goes up.

The eighteenth century is a very important era in the history of landscape gardening. What came to be known as a revolution in gardening taste started at the beginning of the century when people began to react against the formality and stiffness of the French and Dutch gardens. Uh . . . some of the characteristics of these gardens were . . . uh . . . they were very symmetrical, uh   5 . . . they had very axial arrangements, uh the vegetation was carved into very artificial shapes, and this was called the art of topiary, when vegetation was clipped and pruned sometimes into fantastic animal shapes. The bodies of water tended to be very geometrical and it was a very severe discipline that was laid on the landscape, and there was really no regard for the site.   10

The, what came to be known as the English landscape gardening style, in uh contrast to this, its characteristics: there were sweeping lawns, what the English called the greensward, uh a very natural grouping of trees, um . . . winding paths and rivers, the lakes or water bodies had curved edges, and and there was a spontaneity to it. One of the things they always said in   15 reminder or as as a guide was, "Let na . . . nature never be forgot."

*In the next part of the lecture, listen for the pronouns **this** and **it**. Underline each pronoun you hear, and then draw a line to the reference earlier in the section.*

This was brought about for a number of reasons. Historians have have offered a variety of suggestions on why there was this change in perception. For the previous, and this of course occurred over uh several centuries, in in previous times, the landscape that was seen as good or beautiful was a very   20 cultivated landscape, and things like mountains were seen as being very chaotic and um and forests were a place of . . . of hostility, only wild men lived there.

153

In this section, put a box around all the phrases that refer to the situation of the forests.

And progress in civilization was seen more in terms of getting rid of trees, demolishing trees for the cultivated land and as this progressed of course, and England started lo-losing all of their forests uh there became a concern . . . um . . . with this devastation of the land because of course, England was a naval power and to build uh ships, they needed their forests. And some people think it was, one of the influence was John Evelyn's book . . . um . . . entitled *Silva*, that came out in 1664 when he talked about the timber shortage and ways that people could start reforesting England. Also the landed aristocracy, one of the ways they—they they decided to display their wealth was to turn arable land into more of a pleasure ground which was dotted with with trees and this is the era when the country house emerged and the forest and trees were seen . . . were beginning to be seen more as also aesthetic as well as economic. Uh . . . also architectural theories began to suggest the importance of trees as essential to the architectural setting.

*Underline the pronouns **this** and **it** in the next section, and draw a line to the reference.*

And of course, in terms of industrialization, this was when . . . the rise of the city, when London became a very large and polluted city and people began to think of the country as being a place to go for recreation and and it was a type of spiritual renewal.

And so as the advance of of not only the city but also in terms of cultivation people began to want a landscape that was different from this very formal, geometric landscape that they saw all around them. And it was also political, because they saw in the very aristocratic or autocratic control of the landscape the . . . the the French way of doing it and England felt that that in a democratic country that this was not an appropriate style of landscape.

In her conclusion, Major is going to quote someone. Notice how she uses one long sentence to describe the background of the quote. Draw a line down the side of the lines that make up this long sentence. Listen to the pauses in this sentence.

And so what became known as the English landscape style . . . uh I think can be summarized very well. One historian of the period spoke of a gentleman, who was a landscape designer, his name is William Kent, and this is is a very famous line from landscape architectural history, he said that William Kent "leapt the fence and saw that all nature was a garden."

25

30

35

40

45

50

154

Script for Lesson 13

WHY LEAVES CHANGE COLOR
Craig Martin

In the first section of the lecture, Martin rephrases some of his ideas. Underline the original idea and circle the rephrasing.

OK . . . I would like to talk about why leaves change colors . . . uh . . . tree leaves, why they change color in the fall, and . . . uh . . . the various mechanisms . . . that . . . that underlie this change in color and . . . uh . . . some of the . . . environmental conditions, the climatic factors, that influence the change in color.   *5*

Uh . . . it turns out, at the end of the summer, to . . . towards the beginning of the fall, uh . . . there are . . . changes in the environment. The days get shorter, the temperatures get cooler, and many trees respond to these changes by producing hormones. And these hormones cause various compounds in the leaves to break down. In other words, the leaves start to die, as   *10* the trees go dormant. (throat clearing) One of the first things that happens is the green pigment, chlorophyll, disappears and there's a yellow pigment called carotenoid, and tho . . . these yellow pigments, the carotenoids, um . . . appear. They're not synthesized; they're just uncovered by the disappearing chlorophyll, the green pigment. And so, many trees turn yellow, and uh this   *15* again is a result of the disappearance of the green pigment. Other trees, however, turn, well some of these yellow trees are elms and hickories, uh . . . tulip trees in this area, um . . . hackberries do this.

In the next section, Martin speaks very quickly. Draw a line on the left side of any sentence that seems to be spoken very fast.

Other trees, however, turn bright red, and these are the trees most people like to look at. Uh . . . the most popular one is probably the maples. Uh . . .   *20* sumacs do this also, and some trees on campus, that you'll see along roadsides called burning bush, uh . . . are called burning bush for that very reason. They turn bright red. And in these trees, um . . . or shrubs, as the case may be, uh . . . not only does the chlorophyll disappear, and there may be some yellow pigment, the carotenoids, exposed, but there's an actual synthesis of a red   *25* pigment and this red pigment is called anthocyanin . . . antho . . . cyanin. And uh . . . (throat clearing) this synthesis uh again is stimulated by the change in environmental conditions, and the amount of the pigment synthesized is dependent upon the environmental conditions at the precise time . . . um . . . of right before the leaves fall. And this this pigment is synthesized from sugars. So, if it's been a good year for the tree, um . . . in other words, they've photosynthesized a lot, um . . . and they've not been under too much stress, there should be lots of sugar in the leaves. If there's lots of sugar, then there . . . there should be lots of this pigment formed.

In the next section, listen carefully to how much time Martin gives to the syllables in some of his key words. Some of the linking words are also longer to help listeners. This helps listeners follow more easily. If a word sounds longer than normal to you, underline it.

So, first of all, you'll get much brighter red colors if the trees are relatively healthy. But there are other factors involved. Uh . . . the actual conversion of the sugar to the red pigment uh . . . is controlled by various environmental factors. And that conversion uh . . . is influenced by . . . temperature, um and both daytime temperature and nighttime temperature. The uh . . . the warmer the days, the more we get the conversion of the sugars to the . . . to the red pigment . . . and also the cooler the nights uh . . . but not freezing, we can't have freezing conditions because that actually damages the leaves. So warm days followed by cool nights . . . um stimulates (ring) stimulates the synthesis of this red pigment from the sugars.

In this section, Martin continues to talk about environmental factors and he speaks more slowly, sometimes pausing to repeat or emphasize information. Notice the pauses and rephrasing. Underline the key words that Martin stresses.

Um . . . also involved the . . . the . . . the red pigment, the anthocyanin is stimulated by bright sunny days, and so . . . um and this isn't really understood why this occurs, but it does occur. And so, and another thing that's poorly understood, another environmental factor that influences the conversion of sugars to the red pigment, um . . . is . . . a mild drought. In other words, not much water. And so the best conditions to get the bright, the brightest reds in maples, for example, are warm sunny days uh followed by cool nights, and a relatively mild drought, not a severe drought, that's gonna cause the trees to lose their leaves, but a mild drought. And these conditions lead to the best colors.

30

35

40

45

50

In his conclusion, Martin gives an example of one year. He emphasizes adjectives and adverbs to make his points. Circle the adjectives and adverbs that you hear very clearly.

Now it seems to me that uh in several years of observations, that there are   *55*
several plants . . . uh . . . that turn (bright) (red) regardless of the current environmental conditions. Uh . . . maple is not one of these. Uh . . . this particular
fall, uh . . . in 1986, the maples . . . the colors weren't that red. They were
relatively yellow with a slight orange tinge. And uh because conditions were
not as good as, as I've mentioned. Uh . . . we had very wet conditions and   *60*
relatively cold days, and so we had more yellow and slightly orange trees.
They were beautiful, but they weren't very bright red. But there are several
species that don't seem to respond to these environmental factors. And two that
I mentioned previously are the sumac and the . . . uh . . . burning bush. These
two turn brilliant red no matter what. And so they're dependent . . . um re-   *65*
gardless of environmental conditions, they turn bright red. So, that's the story
of of how and the mechanisms and the environmental factors underlying the
change in colors of tree leaves.

Script for Lesson 14

WELLNESS
Wayne H. Osness

As you listen to the tape again, listen for the phrases that reflect academic phrasing. Underline the phrases. On a separate piece of paper, write the phrase in more conversational English.

There's a strong concern today in our society for health and wellness uh . . . among those of us in the United States and around the world. When we talk about health and wellness . . . uh . . . we immediately think about uh . . . handling problems that uh . . . that happen uh . . . in a disease nature. However, we're also concerned about prevention, and those programs that relate to   5
exercise, uh . . . appropriate exercise for given individuals and nutritional programs to make sure that diet is sufficient, uh . . . stress management to reduce the incidence of stress in our lives, and a proper uh . . . choice of personal habits. And so uh . . . health and wellness includes all of those and that . . . we find that it's a very powerful factor in the kinds of illnesses that we can   10
expect.

Also we find in our society today that that uh . . . the cost of health care is uh . . . uh . . . drastically increasing. And uh . . . we must as a nation and within the world do something about that. So we can provide a greater amount of health care for a greater number of people in the world.   15

Also, fortunately uh . . . our scientists have provided a greater uh . . . wealth of information uh . . . from scientific findings indicating the effect of various kinds of intervention strategies uh . . . to the end result. In other words, what can we expect if we do engage in an exercise program or in nu uh . . . ni uh . . . nutrition intervention program. And uh . . . this was heightened   20
by the fact that our Surgeon General recently said in a recent report that 53 percent of the illnesses that we experience today can be avoided using good life-style choices. And so we find that there's a lot that can be done uh . . . by the individual to improve the quality of his life and/or his or her health status. We find that fitness centers are being uh . . . added to uh . . . hospital pro-   25
grams and that the hospitals are now concerned uh . . . with that which happens before. So in a sense our hospitals are working against themselves in that the hospitals would like to keep people well and therefore not need their

services. It's just a difference in the kind of service they provide for our society but certainly one that decreases the trauma associated uh . . . with illness. *30*

In so doing, uh . . . in training individuals, uh . . . we find that our colleges and universities also have to be abreast of this need and to change programs to improve the quality of these programs so that they can in-include uh . . . wellness concepts. And so health educators now are mainly concerned uh . . . with keeping people well as opposed . . . uh . . . to helping after they get sick and the rehabilitation process. We find that during the next decade, our predictors indicate that we're gonna be more concerned with self-responsibility with a concentration on the individual and the quality of life. And so as we look to the this next decade we can find that uh . . . these wellness concepts are gonna be even more important than they are today and *40* so we're gonna need people who are interested in working in this area and we certainly will have an opportunity to improve the quality of life for all people in the world and improve health status to avoid the trauma of illness.

Script for Lesson 15

INTERNATIONAL MONETARY FUND
David E. Shulenburger

As you listen to the tape again, listen for the passive phrases that Shulen-burger used in the lecture, and underline them. On a separate piece of paper, rewrite the sentences containing the passive phrases in your own words.

In 1944 the nations of the world got together and formed the International Monetary Fund. As part of the International Monetary Fund, there was an agreement on the relationship of currencies to one another. Part of the agreement saw the United States, France, and Great Britain define their currencies as key currencies. Defining a currency as a key currency meant that the currency's value was huh . . . defined in terms of gold. The dollar for example was defined such that $35 equaled 1 ounce of gold. The three currencies thus being defined in terms of gold were defined in terms of one another. 5

The remaining countries . . . of the noncommunist world defined their currencies in terms of the key currencies. These countries known as the non-key countries defined currencies in terms of uh . . . the key currencies. Hence, they themselves were defined in terms of one another. This arrangement was an arrangement that was designed to facilitate trade. Any currency was worth gold given the arrangement . . . The initial relationship among . . . huh . . . these currencies was based upon the theory of purchasing power parity. If for example the Mexican peso was initially defined to be worth 8 U.S. cents, that definition was based upon the Mexican peso purchasing in Mexico essentially what 8 U.S. cents would purchase in the United States. While this relationship was a sensible one, it carried with it the seeds of the destruction of the system. 10 15

Following 1944, differential inflation rates occurred among the countries that agreed to be part of this international monetary fund system. Uh . . . for example, if the Mexican economy experienced a 10-percent inflation rate and the U.S. economy experienced a 5-percent inflation rate, that peso in Mexico at the end of 10 years would buy substantially less than would 8 U.S. cents. A natural reaction would be for the citizens of Mexico to wish to convert their pesos to dollars and buy goods in the United States and for U.S. citizens to wish not to buy Mexican goods. They would be too expensive. This has 20 25

160

destabilizing effects on domestic economies. For example, Mexican citizens wishing to buy U.S. goods instead of uh . . . Mexican goods . . . uh . . . cause depression within the Mexican economy. Their attempt to buy U.S. *30* goods in mass causes additional demand in the United States economy and perhaps results in inflation there.

Over the uh . . . period 1944 to 1971, many of these inflation differentials developed among countries and by 1971 there was considerable misalignment among countries causing countries to competitively devalue their currencies in *35* an effort to uh . . . offset these differential rates of inflation. Naturally enough international trade was unpredictable and an individual holding a currency of one country could not be certain next week or next month how much that currency would in fact be worth. Thus, by 1971, Richard Nixon uh . . . had little choice as President of the United States except to abandon the Interna- *40* tional Monetary Fund's fixed rate exchange system and let the dollar freely float with neither gold nor any other guarantee of government fixing its value.

Appendix A

Appendix B

Appendix C

Appendix D

Answering Short Essay Questions

In each lesson, there are a few short essay questions for you to do as review and practice. In an academic class, short essay questions are also more difficult for native speakers because they require more organization of ideas than objective questions do.

When you begin to answer short essay questions, first make sure you understand the question. The following list will help you decide what you need to do to answer the short essay questions in each lesson. You will need this information to complete the discussions and written assignments, too.

Short Essay Questions from the Text	*Suggestions*
1. According to _____, what is the . . . ? (Lesson 8)	Mention a specific point from lecture notes or the text, not your own opinion.
2. Compare . . . (Lessons 3, 7)	Choose two or more ideas and show how they are similar.
3. Consider . . . (Lesson 7)	Think of a problem or issue. Then follow other directions.
4. Define . . . (Lesson 11)	Give the meaning from the lecture or text. Use synonyms for the word. Include the context.
5. Describe . . . (Lessons 1, 4, 5, 9, 14, 15)	Mention the overall purpose or setting of the topic. Include specific details. Create a clear picture in the mind of the reader or listener.
6. Discuss . . . (Lesson 2)	Give a general statement and several details. This may involve your own opinion.
7. Explain the differences . . . (Lesson 7)	Give facts about each situation. Then contrast the details and give the cause of the differences.
8. Explain why . . . (Lessons 4, 11, 12)	Give a reason and support it or prove it with specific details or statistics.

163

Short Essay Questions *from the Text*	*Suggestions*
9. Give the advantages and disadvantages . . . (Lesson 9)	Write about both positive and negative qualities, characteristics, or results. You may need two paragraphs to do this.
10. Give an example . . . (Lessons 1, 13)	Think of a specific situation, experience, or thing. Tell why it is related to the main point.
11. Give a reason or cause . . . (Lessons 3, 12)	Connect a fact or opinion to a result or an effect. Be specific with details of time, place, and process.
12. How does . . . ? (Lesson 13)	Explain the process or method in general and then in detail. Keep the steps in chronological order.
13. List . . . (Lessons 2, 4, 13)	Give the names of items in a group.
List the advantages . . . (Lesson 11)	Tell the positive qualities or results.
List elements . . . (Lesson 5)	Name the components or parts.
List occasions . . . (Lesson 5)	Tell different times when this action takes place.
14. List and tell whether you agree . . . (Lesson 14)	Give examples. Explain your own reaction to the examples. Do you agree or disagree? Explain why briefly.
15. Make a chart . . . (Lesson 9)	Draw a diagram or box. Use this to review different types of information. Divide the diagram or box into smaller areas and label them. Fill in appropriate information in each smaller area.
16. Summarize . . . (Lessons 1, 3, 9)	Include only the main points. Use the main points and subtopics in your notes. Do not use very specific examples. Imagine you are explaining the idea quickly to a friend.
17. Was the . . . effective? (Lesson 15)	Evaluate the facts of the situation. List the goal or plan. Then mention the results. Did they match the goal? Give causes for the results.
18. What are some of the disadvantages . . . ? (Lesson 11)	Concentrate on the problems or the negative results. This may include conditionals or predictions.
19. What are the most common ones? (Lesson 7)	Focus on the ones that were mentioned more than once. Consider those that affect many people or situations.
20. What does _____ recommend? (Lesson 8)	Repeat the lecturer's position or suggestion, not your own opinion.

Suggestions

21. What is the importance of . . . ?
(Lesson 5)

Explain why this concept or object is necessary in a certain context.

22. What is the main difference between . . . ?
(Lesson 12)

Decide which quality or characteristic separates or distinguishes two objects, people, or situations.

23. What is the relationship between . . . ?
(Lesson 13)

Show how two parts are joined or connected. Are they unrelated? Does one cause the other? Is one event or object part of the other? Do they exist together?